WITHDRAWN

Symphony in Steam

THE HISTORY AND DEVELOPMENT OF THE 4-4-0 OR AMERICAN TYPE LOCOMOTIVE

by Jan Gleysteen

Published by TROGON PUBLICATIONS
Scottdale, Pennsylvania

Gift 63072.

HUNTINGTON CITY TOWNSHIP
PUBLIC LIBRARY
255 WEST PARK DRIVE
HUNTINGTON, IN 46750

Copyright © 1966 by Jan Gleysteen, Scottdale, Pa. 15683
Printed in the United States of America

Library of Congress Catalog Card Number: 66-17851

Second, revised edition, 1970.

To Linda Jo and Richard David

Foreword

A book about one single type of steam locomotive suggests a highly specialized presentation, but those even slightly acquainted with the subject of this volume know better. The wonder is not that a book should be published about the "American"-type locomotive but that we have had to wait so long for someone to record the story of this masterpiece of locomotive design which over the course of a century established itself as the classic symbol of a new society.

If ever a nation had a love affair with a product of its own ingenuity, the United States had one with the locomotive we designate technically as the 4-4-0. In innumerable ways it worked magic in the hearts of millions of Americans over five generations and earned naturally the name which common affection bestowed on it—the "American" type. Thus we have here not only the story of a magnificent steam locomotive but also the exciting response of an energetic and turbulent society to its most cherished mechanical creation.

People require many kinds of symbols to see and grasp firmly their own qualities and aspirations. They commonly select famous men, places, and events to exemplify what they value. In this elite company the "American" locomotive finds itself very much at home, because its own qualities emerged from and mirrored comparable qualities of the society it served. In short, the American-type person built his own traits into the American-type steam locomotive. That is why he loved it.

Consider for a moment just a few of the thoughts which a reading of this volume will bring imperceptibly to the forefront of the mind. Mobility, especially the wish to move with speed, has always distinguished the American from other societies. The steam locomotive gratified the urge for movement, and the American-type locomotive beyond all others sang the song of speed. From start to finish the 4-4-0's produced new speed records, whether interurban, transcontinental, or in measured miles per hour. When old "999" won immemorial fame as the fastest thing on wheels, the whole world cheered. The close association between a mobile, impatient society and the 4-4-0's emerges clearly from the simple fact that the American-type locomotive outnumbered all its rivals by thousands and became the national favorite. It typified speed, a quality valued by the people.

It also typified mechanical ingenuity, or what some called "Yankee" ingenuity. The product of experiment, it became also the subject of experiment. Some ideas tried out on the 4-4-0's, like the air brake, brought lasting benefits to railroading; others earned such titles as "Holman's Absurdity." But tinkering, altering, inventing, and improving—qualities dear to the American people—centered on the American-type locomotive if only because there were so many of them so widely distributed. For several generations these remarkable engines represented the highest level of mechanical perfection of their age. They brought a thrill of fulfillment to those who vicariously shared pride in their meticulous craftsmanship. Mid-century gems like the "John C. Breckinridge," the "William Mason," or the silver engine called "America" proved without any question the skill, indeed the genius, of the mechanic arts in the United States.

The American people admire functional ideas. They like things that work well or promise some improvement. In this sense the 4-4-0 locomotive gave expression to a pervasive national spirit. A jack-of-all-trades, the American type doubled in passenger and freight service; it had speed for the plains and power for the mountain hauls; it had water and fuel capacity for long runs and the quick starting needed for short-line service; it required little routine maintenance, and ran incredible distances between overhauls; and it had a durability which made companies measure its life-span by quarter centuries rather than decades. Simply

5

designed, it proved adaptable, economical, and dependable. It is no wonder that a practical, thrifty people should have formed an attachment to this practical, thrifty locomotive.

But some elements of the spirit of Americans lie a good deal deeper than their predilection for speed, mechanical devices, and practical efficiency. They love high adventure, and respond eagerly to the episodes of danger, of violence, and of heroism which give excitement to history and zest to folklore. The 4-4-0's played a major role in many of the classic adventure tales of the nation, from the Great Locomotive Chase to the career of Jesse James. It is fascinating to see in how many of these thrillers the American locomotive played a central role in the drama.

And finally, the American people have always been individualists. Despite their progress toward a uniformity born of mass production, they have always craved to impress some mark of individuality upon objects they possess. Skilled craftsmanship in wood and metal has appealed to them as an art form more than painting or music.

On no product of the nineteenth century did designers and workmen lavish more loving care than on the railroad locomotives of that era. They were more than melodies in metal or symphonies in steel. Each had its distinctive name and its unique personality. The 4-4-0's achieved so glorious a union between function and form that they became literally objects of art to the society which had created them. The trim lines of the boiler, banded with brass and resplendent with bright enamel; the ornately painted headlight, cylinders, and domes; the roomy cab, a marvel of cabinetmaking emblazoned with the identifying name; the racy running gear with wheels painted scarlet; and the whole locomotive and tender delicately pinstriped and embellished with Spencerian flourishes in gold—this mechanical marvel, when it came to life with stentorian exhaust, flashing side-rods and swirling smoke and steam, spelled the word "beauty" to the contemporary beholder.

For this reason, more than any of the others, I am glad that the story of the 4-4-0 American locomotive has been written by Jan Gleysteen, for he is primarily an artist. He has, to be sure, painted a broad canvas. He has preserved the essential record with a richness of information and anecdote that will engage the interest of all kinds of people, whether historians or folklorists, serious modelers or dilettante hobbyists, live-steam buffs or professional railroadmen, armchair tourists or those on the road, philatelists or print collectors, photographers or designers, illustrators or bibliophiles. Mr. Gleysteen's own drawings and his selection of prints will evoke in us, as only the artist's hand can do, the feelings of wonder and pride and excitement which the 4-4-0's inspired in the people of their day. It may, indeed, be true that every new material creation of mankind, in its course from invention to obsolescence, passes through a stage in which it attains its peak of perfection as functional art. As McKay's clipper ships marked this point in the evolution of sailing vessels, so the 4-4-0 American type reached the apex of artistic perfection in the era of the steam locomotive.

I am pleased that Mr. Gleysteen asked me to do the foreword for this book. I do not know whether he settled on me because I am an American historian or because I once, in an unguarded moment, confided to him that I had fallen under the spell of the 4-4-0, Pennsylvania's D16a, at the age of four. Its 80-inch drivers then looked as tall as a house to me, and its high stack towered majestically to the sky. This vivid recollection of my first sight of a 4-4-0 made my punishment for running away from home to look at the trains seem insignificant indeed.

Jan Gleysteen has ideal qualifications to prepare a book on the 4-4-0's. He draws from a deep reservoir of experience as illustrator, designer, and artist to create a thorough and beautiful presentation of this famous locomotive type. He has woven the essential facts into an exciting narrative, full of human interest. He has carefully preserved, in word and picture, an important record which, as the reader will discover, is stored with surprises. He has ranged widely, from the first inventors to the final enumeration of all 4-4-0's known to exist today and from the men who once held the throttle to those who ride only the train of memory. This book catches more than the spirit of old "999"; it catches the spirit of the people who made and idolized her 25,600 sisters. It celebrates the 4-4-0 locomotive, that American beauty with whom a whole nation fell in love.

Philip Shriver Klein
Professor of American History
The Pennsylvania State University

CONTENTS

0–4–0 FOUR WHEEL SWITCHER

0–4–0t

0–6–0t

2–8–0 CONSOLIDATION

4-4-0 AMERICAN

Jan Gleysteen

2–4–4t

2–6–2t

2–8–2 MIKADO

2–6–4t

2–8–4 BERKSHIRE or KANAWHA

4–4–2 ATLANTIC

2–10–2t

4–8–2t

4–8–2 MOUNTAIN

2–4–2 COLUMBIA

4–6–6–2t

2–8–8–2t

4–8–4 NORTHERN or NIAGARA

0–6–0 SIX WHEEL SWITCHER

PRINCIPAL TYPES OF
STEAM LOCOMOTIVES

(WHEEL COUNT STARTS AT FRONT Engines not drawn to scale)

2–10–0 DECAPOD

2–6–0 MOGUL

2–10–2 SANTA FE

4–4–4–4 DUPLEX–

2–6–2 PRAIRIE

4–4–6–4 DUPLEX

4–10–0 MASTODON

4–6–0 TEN WHEELER

2–6–6–2

4–10–2 SOUTHERN PACIFIC or SUPER MOUNTAIN

2–6–4 ADRIATIC

4–6–6–4 CHALLENGER

2–10–4 TEXAS

4–6–2 PACIFIC

2–6–6–6 ALLEGHENY

4–12–2 UNION PACIFIC

4–6–4 HUDSON

2–10–10–2 VIRGINIAN

2–8–8–2 BEYER GARRATT

0–8–0 EIGHT WHEEL SWITCHER

4–8–8–4 BIG BOY, world's largest locomotive

4–8–8–2 CAB FORWARD ARTICULATED

8

CHAPTER ONE

Campbell's Contribution

A cool drizzle descended on the two-car special that was about to depart from Springfield, Illinois, early on the morning of February 11, 1861. Heading the two yellow coaches was the wood burner "L. M. Wiley," an early 4-4-0-type locomotive. A tall man with a stovepipe hat addressed the few neighbors and friends that had braved the elements to see him off on his journey: "My friends"—the words seem to echo now in that familiar high-pitched voice—"no one not in my situation can appreciate my feelings of sadness at this parting. To this place, and the kindness of these people, I owe everything. Here I have lived a quarter of a century, and have passed from a young to an old man. I now leave, not knowing when, or whether ever, I may return." A few minutes later Abraham Lincoln, the country lawyer from Illinois, was on his way to Washington to become our nation's sixteenth President. The train trip of 1,900 miles took twelve days over twenty-two different railroads. Today this distance can be traveled in less than one day over a single road, the Baltimore & Ohio.

The words spoken on that wintry morning found their answer four years later. In the early dawn of a gorgeous spring day, May 3, 1865, the funeral train of the beloved President, consisting of seven coaches painted black, moved into Springfield after a ride of thirteen days over thirteen railroads. This trip from Washington, D.C., by way of Philadelphia and New York, West Point and Albany, Cleveland and Columbus, required the use of twenty-six engines, and interestingly, every one of the locomotives was a wood-burning 4-4-0 or American type.

This was no mere coincidence. Had the railroads chosen twenty-six other engines from their roster, more than likely these would all have been 4-4-0's also. At the turn of the century, the popular 4-4-0 locomotive had been in use longer than any other type of engine. It was built in greater numbers than any other kind of

locomotive until increased weight and speed began to take their toll. In the old days the American types handled everything beyond the yard limits; whether plush limiteds or fast freights, main line trains or mixed locals.

The first 4-4-0 was built by James Brooks of Philadelphia in 1836 for the Philadelphia & Germantown R.R. The last ones for the domestic market were built by Baldwin for the Chicago and Illinois Midland in 1928— 92 years later! These C. & I.M. engines quit running in March 1954, ending 118 years of 4-4-0 service over the main lines. Meanwhile other American types continued to serve the short lines as late as 1962 (Winnipeg Hydro, Louisiana Eastern, Mississippi Central). They were a hardy breed indeed!

For those who may not be acquainted with locomotive classification, an explanation is in order. Any engine with a four-wheel lead truck (4), four driving wheels (4), and not having a trailing truck (0) is known as a 4-4-0, or named American-type locomotive. An engine of later design with two leading wheels, eight drivers, and a four-wheel trailing truck is classified as a 2-8-4, or Berkshire. Any locomotive with the same wheel arrangement would have the same classification and name. Exceptions would be the 4-8-4 Northern, which is also known as Niagara, and the Mikado which was rechristened MacArthur in the war against Japan. However, this new name never stuck. This book deals exclusively with the American type.

The first engines were generally four-wheel types of which either one pair of wheels or all four wheels were drivers. Examples are the granddaddy of all iron horses, Stephenson's "Rocket" of 1827, which had two drivers, and the "Stourbridge Lion" (1829), the "Best Friend of Charleston" (1830), the "John Bull," and the "DeWitt Clinton" (1831), all of which were four-wheel-driven engines. The first stage of transition away from the four-wheel locomotives came when the

9

Baltimore and Ohio R.R. received the first of eight "one-arm-Billys." This was a 4-2-0 locomotive named "Lafayette," the world's first engine with a lead truck. Because this truck helped guide the engine into the curve of the track, the new locomotives did not derail as frequently as the earlier models.

No road, it is generally conceded, did more to encourage locomotive research and development than the Penn State Rail Road. Yet when Coleman Sellers and Sons offered them a plan for a 4-4-0 in 1834, they turned it down as too revolutionary. Even Mathias Baldwin, the Philadelphia watchmaker who had constructed "Old Ironsides" and more than a hundred later engines, regarded the innovation with distrust. But in spite of the disclaimers, Henry Campbell, also of Philadelphia, took out patents on a 4-4-0 type locomotive in 1836 and persuaded someone to build one for him. So it was in 1836 that James Brooks (not to be confused with the later Horatio Brooks, of the Brooks Locomotive Works, Dunkirk, New York) produced in thirteen months' time the first 4-4-0. It was bought by the Philadelphia and Germantown R.R., a predecessor of the present-day Reading R.R. The rough-riding contraption had trouble keeping all eight wheels in touch with the strap iron track of those days. But within the first year of operation a Mr. Harrison of the firm of Garrett & Eastwick corrected this deficiency by inventing the equalizing beam (U.S. Patent No. 700), which remained virtually unchanged on all 4-4-0's and larger locomotives built since. Acting on the principle that a three-legged stool will stand firmly on any surface, no matter how uneven, Joseph Harrison, Jr., came up with a system which suspended the weight of the engine over three points. Recognized as one of the greatest improvements ever made in locomotive design, the equalizing beam helps an engine to run smoothly over rough or curvy tracks. As a result of this invention the 4-4-0 became so popular that it was soon referred to as the American Standard Type or American for short.

One of Eastwick & Harrison's (Harrison was made a partner in the business in 1839) 4-4-0's was the "Gowan & Marx" built for the Philadelphia and Reading, which came up with an outstanding performance for its time. On February 20, 1840, it hauled 101 cars of freight from Reading to Philadelphia, with a payload of 423 long tons, or forty times its own weight, at a speed of ten miles per hour. The Philadelphia & Reading R.R. was understandably proud of this record and ordered a dozen more engines of this same class built. What is thought to be one of these famous engines has miraculously survived. The oldest 4-4-0 in existence, known as the People's Railway No. 3, was retired in 1883, but escaped the torch and was presented to the Franklin Institute in Philadelphia in 1933. It is similar to the "Gowan & Marx," but has a longer wheelbase. The cab and headlight now on it were obviously added later.

Eastwick and Harrison, who built the "Gowan & Marx," were appointed by Czar Nicholas I to construct more than one hundred locomotives for Russia's first important railroad, connecting Moscow with St. Petersburg (now Leningrad). Rather than ship all the locomotives from the States, which seemed impractical to them, Eastwick and Harrison moved their shop and equipment to Russia where they reopened under the name of Alexandroffsky Head Mechanical Works.

As the demand for eight-wheelers increased some thirty-five or more firms began building them. Soon countless 4-4-0's were emerging from machine shops in the industrial Eastern states. In Paterson, N.J., alone, four separate shops were producing Americans. In addition to Brooks and Eastwick & Harrison we now find such time-honored names as Rogers, Mason, Danforth Cooke, Grant, Norris and Sons, Hinkley, Amoskeag, Taunton, Lawrence, and McQueen, all involved in building 4-4-0's. Besides, numerous railroads built

Americans in their home shops, and so homemade 4-4-0's joined the rosters of the Pennsylvania R.R., Union Pacific, Wabash, Louisville and Nashville, to mention just a few.

But pioneer builder Mathias Baldwin was still unconvinced. He experimented with a number of other designs, such as the six- and eight-wheel connected freight engines, with a flexible beam arrangement for lateral movement. As a result Baldwin lost a number of customers to other builders. But finally in 1845 he agreed to build a number of 4-4-0's for the South Carolina Canal and Rail Road Company. Baldwin then managed to secure patent rights from Henry Campbell and from Eastwick & Harrison for the equalizing beam, and delivered his first 4-4-0's to the South Carolina Canal & Rail Road Company before the end of the year. With the delivery of these engines Baldwin's feelings changed dramatically. Now he was as much in favor of the American type as he once had been prejudiced against it. He commented on one occasion that he "was more pleased with the appearance and performance of the 4-4-0 than with any engine he had ever turned out." Baldwin completed only one more six-wheel connected engine. From that time on the 4-4-0 took the No. 1 spot in the Baldwin catalog. He turned them out in larger numbers than the ten-wheelers, Moguls, and single-drivered engines, which were also offered for sale at the Baldwin Locomotive Works.

In 1862, to take just one year, Baldwin produced 4-4-0's not only for the domestic market but also for the Veronej-Rostoff R.R. in Russia, the Dom Pedro Segundo Railway of Brazil, the New South Wales and Queensland Railways in Australia, and the first locomotives for the Finnish Railways. Altogether some 150 other shops, about evenly divided between commercial enterprises and railroad-owned operations (such as the Pennsylvania's Altoona Works), eventually produced 25,600 locomotives with the 4-4-0 wheel arrangement! This was 8,000 more engines than the number of ten-wheelers built, the next popular type. Only in the last days of steam did the Consolidation type, 2-8-0, finally outnumber the 4-4-0 by 5,900 units. This was mainly because of the large export orders to Italy, China, Romania, Belgium, and orders for the United States Army Transportation Corps and the UNRRA, during and after the two wars. On the home front the 4-4-0 continued to lead by a safe margin.

As a result this locomotive, used on practically every railroad in the United States and Canada, was the archetypical engine as long as steam survived. It possessed all the necessary features to meet the rugged demands of an expanding America, and yet was pos-

sibly the simplest and most accessible engine ever built. One peculiar characteristic of the 4-4-0 design was the feeling of openness and lightness, created by the amount of air visible beneath the boiler between the pilot wheels and the drivers. She was not only a graceful product, but a leading lady in the drama of this continent's development. The 4-4-0 helped win the Civil War, and opened up the great West. It radically changed the traveling and shipping customs of this nation. Take any book on the Civil War, study the history of most any state in our nation, or the provinces to the north, visit any railroad museum, and you will find an abundant evidence of the American-type's prominence.

Since 4-4-0's pulled the first trains to reach many a new area for decades on end, and were the first locomotives to cross rivers and open up new territories, it is much easier to list exceptions than to chronicle all the areas the 4-4-0 served. Only a few 4-4-0's were used in the Colorado Rockies, which were from the beginning a paradise of Consolidations and Mikados. With the exception of the Mount Gretna Railroad in Central Pennsylvania, the two-foot gauge lines in the United States did not use 4-4-0's. The Mt. Gretna Line had three Baldwin-built 4-4-0's, one of which was built in the record time of eight days starting from raw materials! And finally 4-4-0's were notably absent from the logging railroads. John T. Labbe, author of "Railroads in the Woods," claims that logging roads using 4-4-0's often had hopes of obtaining common carrier status, though they seldom achieved it.

Perhaps the one outstanding feature of the American was its inherent simplicity, resulting in efficient and dependable operation. Again and again we read glowing testimonies from the master mechanics regarding their American types. The records speak for themselves. One Pennsylvania Railroad American type was in constant service from September 9, 1867, to May 14, 1871, covering 153,280 miles without time off for repairs. A Baldwin-built 4-4-0, No. 96 of the Wisconsin Central, a McQueen type delivered in 1886, made 891 trips in two years and nine months on passenger trains No. 5 and 6, covering 136,500 miles, without being late once, and without need for repairs. No. 96 continued to serve the line for 42 years.

The Pennsy, which as late as 1911 had nearly half its roster in 4-4-0's, operated a D 16a (built in 1895) on the Middle Division for three years and four months without repairs. The only defect they could find was that the wheels showed 8/32 inch wear. No wonder then that this most 4-4-0-minded road even rebuilt some larger types, such as Moguls, and practically all of its famous Stevens engines into Americans!

CHAPTER TWO

Melodies in Metal

Locomotives, unlike automobiles, developed logically and did not try to imitate a previous form of transportation, such as a horse-drawn carriage. This was an advantage. Form followed function, which is still the basis for good design. However, the first locomotives were no objects of beauty. Since each engine was essentially a one-of-a-kind experiment (the grasshopper type, horizontal- and vertical-boilered engines, eight-wheel connected flexible beam types, etc.), there was no accumulated knowledge to draw upon, and no need for uniformity and interchangable parts. All parts were made by hand, with simple tools. This required patience, skill, and good judgment by the individual craftsman. Once a satisfactory wheel arrangement was found in the 4-4-0 and the later Moguls (2-6-0's), some attention could be given to details, refinements, and innovations. Even though each engine was still largely custom built, increased knowledge and better means of production resulted in more efficient and dependable locomotives.

The next decades were not characterized by the appearance of many new types, but rather by the improvement of the existing ones. We have already mentioned the three-point suspension device which opened the way to greater speed and capacity. Around 1840 a beginning was made in the use of counterweights on the drivers. The next item to be studied and standardized was the valve gear. Looking over old prints in locomotive catechisms, we see that an endless array of steam-distribution systems had come into use, but during the middle 1900's the Stephenson link motion became the favorite. It was invented by William Williams, an employee of the Stephenson Company at Newcastle in England, and was first used on the British locomotives in 1842. The Stephenson innovation was first applied to an American engine, a Rogers 4-4-0 named "Victory," in 1849. For the Stephenson valve gear it was a lasting victory indeed!

Another thing the old prints reveal is that both inside and outside cylinder engines were built during the 1840's and the 50's. Each type had its own advantages. Inside cylinder engines run steadier on short wheel-base locomotives such as the American type, because cylinders located outside have greater leverage to shunt the entire locomotives from side to side. There is less heat loss than when the cylinders are exposed. Also, engines take up less lateral room, which is a decided advantage on mountainous runs with tunnels and bridges.

However, outside cylinders are more accessible for maintenance, inspection, and repairs. American practice favored the ease of maintenance and the possibility of larger cylinders over smooth running, while the British and European plants continued to build large fleets of excellent-running inside-cylinder 4-4-0's. In addition three-cylinder engines were built both here and abroad with one cylinder between and two outside the frame, each cylinder cranked 120°, or one third from the others.

The earliest locomotives, including the first 4-4-0's, being built by hand, had a life-span of only ten to fifteen years. And since the first railroad photo wasn't taken until 1851 (a daguerrotype of the British South Eastern Railway No. 136, a 4-2-0 named "Folkestone"), we rely heavily on old accounts, woodcut illustrations, and the Currier and Ives prints for information. And some of the information that reaches us out of the dim past does not quite match other bits of information.

Consider the case of the locomotive cab. The first engineers stood on an open deck that rocked and swayed along at the outlandish speed of fifteen or even twenty miles per hour. The pioneers of this new form of transportation endured not only the aromatic smoke of their wood-burning steeds, but the driving snow and rain, or the merciless heat of the summer sun as well. The need for some form of protection was felt by all men on the iron road, and some added their own parasols to the engine.

Since the cab was such an inevitable addition, mothered by necessity, we now have at least three sources reporting the first cab. A simple wooden and tarpaulin shelter was built over the grasshopper-type locomotive, "Samuel P. Ingham" of the Beaver Meadow Railroad in Pennsylvania. From another source we find a tarpaulin cover of some kind on a Western Railroad of Massachusetts engine in 1841. The first enclosed cab was credited to Joseph Davenport, engineer on the old Boston and Providence line in 1843. The management frowned on such a comfortable place to "loaf in" for their crews. "Next we'll have to give them something to sit down on!" (And they did.)

The cab soon found general approval, and Baldwin, Rogers, Hinkley, Norris, and Grant began to deliver engines with a roof already in place. The People's Railway (Philadelphia and Reading) was the first railroad to specifically order roofs on seventeen locomotives delivered in 1846. These engines were also the first on which Baldwin placed sandboxes. The wooden roofs were supported by four iron posts, to which the enginemen themselves added curtains. The People's Railway No. 3 (see description page 10) may also have acquired its first cab at this time.

Twenty years later the cabs reached their height of glory. Fine oak, mahogany, black walnut, and bird's-eye maple were used in their construction. Even during the Civil War, when time for construction was at a premium, 4-4-0's for the military railroads were delivered with curved-glass windows, upholstered seat boxes, shadowed lettering, and meticulous pinstriping.

In 1859 James Milholland, master engineer of the Philadelphia and Reading, designed the first metal cab, which oddly enough was round-walled and dome-topped. A 4-4-0 built by Rogers in 1889 for the Long Island Railroad had a wooden cab with a steel extension extending well over the tender. This led to the introduction of the first all-steel cab in 1895 on the Lehigh Valley Railroad.

As the rails moved out from the cities and longer lines connected with other lines beyond, night operation became an unavoidable necessity. Horatio Allen's famous but rather dangerous attempt to light up the track ahead with a bonfire on a sand-loaded flatcar two cars ahead of the engine was superseded by a real oil-burning headlight sometime between 1840 and 1850. First reports on headlights come from the Boston and Worcester and the Mad River and Lake Erie roads. By 1850 the familiar box-shaped headlights were in fairly general use. Around 1870 the lights on the 4-4-0's were usually bought separately from an independent manufacturer such as the Kelly Lamp Works, Post and Co., Adams and Westlake (still in business), or Foster and Co. They were boxes about two feet square and eighteen inches deep, topped by a ventilator half again as high. Mounted on ornate scrollwork brackets, they were frequently decorated with paintings of landscapes or animals, portraits of Presidents and ladies, scrolls, and Pennsylvania Dutch designs. These traveling art galleries at times had a nice set of deer antlers added for good measure.

The locomotive whistle, another optional extra in those days, came to us from England. Its melodious tones, heard by generations with deep emotions ranging from nostalgia to wanderlust, have added such a major element of romance to railroading. In 1833, after a grade-crossing accident in which the locomotive "Sampson" scrambled a load of butter and eggs, a device known as a steam trumpet was added to the "Comet," a sister engine. In the United States the locomotive "Sandusky" of the Mad River and Lake Erie may have been the first engine to be equipped with a whistle. The railroad's president was so impressed with the instrument that the locomotive ran out of steam several times, having used it all on a rather monotonous concert.

In our time an engineer on a Class I railroad may be assigned to a different engine each time he makes a run. But in the heyday of the eight-wheeler, the company would assign an engine to its own engineer, who with his crew was held responsible for its appearance. Like a captain on his own ship the engineer would take personal command of his engine on each run, unless it was laid up for repairs. When an engineer received a new locomotive, he would add his own whistle and lantern to it—especially the whistle. This was the engineer's personal property which went with him as he changed locomotives or employment. Engineers took pride in tuning their large, sweet-sounding chime whistles and developed an individual style of blowing them.

Naturally the engineers were very proud of their machines. No matter how long or tiring the run they would always find time to keep them in A-1 shape. Henry Ward Beecher, the famous preacher from Brooklyn, once remarked that he loved to go past the enginehouse "to see the sons of industry pet their entrusted engines with loving care." After each run every last smudge of soot was cleaned from boiler and drivers. Domes, cylinders, bands, and fittings were highly polished, and the paint was never allowed to become chipped or faded.

Many engineers who had proven their worth to their company were allowed to have their names painted on the cab sides, often in gold lettering or ornate script. One engineer, Charles H. Grant, was very proud of his American type, No. 21 on the Wabash, and spent much effort on its maintenance. When the Wabash sold this locomotive to California's Yosemite Valley Line, he was asked to deliver it. Upon arrival he found it hard to part from old 21. So he wrote a note of regret to the Wabash and hired out to the Y.V. instead. His name stayed under the window sash for the rest of his active life.

Between 1850 and 1870 the 4-4-0's passed through their most decorative period. A maroon engine with lots of brass trim, bright red drivers and cowcatcher, Prussian blue panels on cab and tender, shaded gold leaf stars, lettering, and numbers was quite in harmony with the rococo tastes of the era, consistent with the gingerbread and trim on the houses of that time. Perhaps the gaudiest engine ever constructed was the 4-4-0 "Wyoming," built in Philadelphia in 1857. This engine was almost completely covered with bright scrollwork, flashing brass eagles and stars, portraits and shields in a cacophony of colors. It also had five arch windows with cut glass on each side!

Much more restrained, and considerably more beautiful, was the locomotive "America," better known as the "Silver Engine." Built by the Grant Locomotive Works of Paterson, New Jersey, its boiler was covered with fine German silver. And all the trim—cab handles, whistle, flay staffs, and headlight supports—were of pure silver. After being exhibited at the Exposition International de Paris in 1867, it was bought by the Rock Island for passenger service. It was again exhibited in Philadelphia in 1876. The locomotive industry had progressed from the crude, utilitarian, one-of-a-kind engine to mass-produced stock locomotives, individualized and decorated by the buyers with a great deal of thought. One designer's name towers above that of his contemporaries: William Mason of Taunton, Massachusetts.

William Mason, builder of cotton mill machinery, saw a locomotive demonstration in 1852 at Lowell, Massachusetts. He was so impressed by the performance of the "Eddy Clock" engine, "Addison Gilmore," that three months later he decided to enter the railroad business himself. Mason was not only an excellent mechanic, but also had an eye for beauty. He declared that locomotives "ought to look better than cookstoves on wheels," and every detail he designed showed a marked degree of improvement. Yet Mason sacrificed not a single degree of usefulness and efficiency in his engines. In many ways he was ahead of his time, and his engines were often imitated by other builders. Mason was the first to use the Walschaert valve gear in the United States in 1876, but the American railroads were not quite ready for it at that time. Mason's 4-4-0's were described by Mathias Forney as "melodies cast and wrought in metal." The "Highland Light," a locomotive he built for the Cape Cod Central in 1867, is by many regarded as the acme in locomotive design as practiced in the 1860's.

Thirty-one years after the demonstration at Lowell, Mason had turned out 713 locomotives, and it was at that time that he literally gave his life for a locomotive. By the end of 1883 he finished the last one of a series of 4-4-0 locomotives for the Columbus and Eastern Railroad. Whether the C. & E. was unable to make the payments we don't know, but for some reason the delivery of this engine was held back. Some time later the Old Colony Railroad, now a part of the New Haven, bought the engine.

In the transaction it had been overlooked that the C. & E. used vacuum brakes, and the Old Colony used Westinghouse Air Brakes. Mason sent a crew over to make the change and he arrived at the Taunton enginehouse later. Since the Old Colony wanted the engine in a hurry, William Mason threw off his coat and worked right along with his men. He worked up a sweat, suffered a chill, and shortly thereafter died of pneumonia. So 4-4-0 No. 11 of the Old Colony cost Mason his life.

Jan Gleystoen/66

CHAPTER THREE

Coal Burners and Camelbacks

Among the mightiest engines that thundered across the Mojave Desert and fought their way up and through the high Sierras were Southern Pacific's unique cab-forward articulateds, 4-8-8-2's. There are many tunnels on Southern Pacific's "Route over the Hill" and about forty miles of snow sheds, too. When a locomotive of normal design entered one of the tunnels, it was as one engineer described it, "as if all hell had broke loose." The hot fumes of the exhaust reduced the crews' visibility and oxygen to a dangerous minimum. The men were issued respirators, covering nose and mouth, but this was not a practical solution.

In 1910 the designers of the Baldwin Locomotive Works and Southern Pacific's mechanical engineers solved the problem by building a series of oil-burning locomotives, eventually 256 in all, that were turned hind side forward, with the tender following what once had been the front. The exhaust problem had been brought under control with an engine that "backed up to go forward."

Now what did these giants of the West have in common with a 4-4-0? At first glance you might conclude: nothing but the track they run on. But wait a minute! The very first cab-forward was a 4-4-0, built in 1900 at the Sausalito shops of the narrow-gauge North Pacific Coast Railroad. No. 21 was rebuilt from the remains of an earlier engine, N.P.C. No. 5. Her cab was set over the cylinders, and she was followed by a flatcar with two tanks, one for oil and the other for water. Although the engine was officially named "Thomas Stetson," the crew named her "The Freak," which was more descriptive. "The Freak" served for a while on the Cazadero passenger run, but in the fourth year of service someone let the water get low and its tubes were burnt. The engine was dismantled and the boiler, once repaired, was sold to a steam laundry.

This is only one of the numerous instances in which the 4-4-0 made a lasting contribution by offering a historic first. Readily available, they were a natural for experiments and innovations.

The first locomotives, 4-4-0's as well as others, were wood burners. The amount of fuel these old engines used was almost unbelievable. On a fairly level railroad each engine consumed about 1,550 cords annually. Now a cord of wood is a pile four feet wide by four feet high by eight feet long. We must admire the fireman of those days for shoving 1,550 such piles into the firebox of his engines every twelve months. One railroad, the New York, Ogdensburg, and Lake Champlain, later named Rutland, bought 46,000 cords of wood per year for its thirty engines. This would make a pile four feet high by seventy miles long.

Engineers were furnished with fuel checks or brass tokens for their run. When an engine was about to run out of fuel (the old tenders held only two or three cords of wood), the engineer would stop at a farm and exchange a ticket for each one half cord of wood he took. One some roads, after the crew had wooded up, the fuel checks were countersigned and left in a wooden box provided for that purpose. The farmer of the woodlot would periodically cash the tickets and tokens at the nearest depot. The account department would then charge the fuel and other supplies (such as a quart of lard oil, also from the farm) to the operating expenses of the engine named on the ticket. Wooding up normally took about half an hour, but often on passenger trains the men and boys would come up front to help. With a long journey still ahead, they were glad enough to save the time and welcomed the exercise.

But in 1852 the Hudson River Railroad, now part of the New York Central, introduced the 4-4-0 locomotive "Irvington" as the first to burn coal. Like many innovations, this was met with some distrust, even though industrial plants had used coal for years. The principal

15

objections were the residue of hard cinders, and that a coal fire, while hotter, needs more constant attention. Finally, after these objections were overcome, coal burners came into general use. For many years, though, wood and coal burners operated side by side, with the wood burners converted to coal burners during their next general overhaul. Two years later, in 1854, the Pennsylvania Railroad was the first line to use firebrick deflectors in the firebox.

In the 1930's the conversion process was reversed by the twenty-three-mile Collins and Glenville Railroad in Georgia. The short line had bought two old locomotives. Since wood was easier to come by than coal in that region, a few changes were made, and diamond stacks with spark arrestors were added. On a diet of cottonwood, they continued to roll until the line itself went out of business.

Steel tires were first introduced on a series of locomotives built by Baldwin in 1862 for the Dom Pedro Segundo Railway of Brazil. Steel boilers came into use six years later.

In 1900 the first streamlined train, the F. U. Adams Windsplitter, was tested on the Baltimore and Ohio Railroad at Relay, Maryland. It was pulled by an ordinary nonstreamlined American type. The tests "proved" that streamlining was a waste of effort and money, and the idea was shelved, in the United States, at least, for another thirty-three years.

The available pictures show the Adams Windsplitter from the rear, circumstantial evidence that the 4-4-0 up front was not in matching style. It could have been, though. In 1865 Samuel L. Calthrop of Roxbury, Massachusetts, constructed a model of a streamlined American type to accompany his patent application for an "air-resisting" train as he called it. The patent (No. 49227, Reg. U.S. Pat. Off.) included full-width diaphrams and enclosed drop steps. But Calthrop, unsuccessful in selling his idea, was clearly too far ahead of his time!

In 1866 an idea was born that, while closely connected with railroads, was clearly not beneficial to the carriers or their passengers. During the night of October 6, 1866, the Reno brothers held up the eastbound passenger train of the Ohio and Mississippi Valley Railroad and made off with the safe and parcels from the Adams Express car immediately behind the wood-burning 4-4-0. The safe with $30,000 was abandoned in pursuit, but the packages containing $15,000 presumably went along to Iowa with the Renos. Two of the brothers came back to Indiana in 1867, and again held up the train, this time acquiring $8,000. Since it was now rather unhealthy for the Renos to reside in Indiana, they "worked" their way to Council Bluffs,

Iowa, where they were captured. All escaped from jail and returned to Indiana once more, where they held up a Jefferson, Madison, and Indianapolis Railroad train at Marshfield, which netted them $90,000. This time they killed the express messenger.

The Reno brothers found no security in their profession, for the Citizens' Vigilante Committee finished their career in 1868. A farmer found them swaying in the breeze from the branches of his beech tree, and one member of the gang received a twenty-five-year lease on a small room. Nevertheless, the idea of robbing trains had caught on and continued to plague the railroads till well in the 20th century. The first train robbery in the West took place at Verdi, Nevada, on November 4, 1870. The train from which the Wells Fargo safe was relieved of $41,000 in coins and bullion was also pulled by an eight-wheeled wood burner.

To counteract this evil, at least one 4-4-0 served on the side of law and order. When at the turn of the century Butch Cassidy's gang was terrorizing Wyoming, Union Pacific's special agent Keliher had engine 845 attached to a converted baggage car equipped with bunk beds, kitchen, and horse stalls. When word was received of a robbery, the sheriffs and their rangers, horses and all, took off after them by train. Stopping at the closest point to the desperadoes' probable whereabouts, the posse lowered gangplanks and was on its way. Needless to say, Cassidy was not equal to such mobilization.

The year 1869 is a date that deserves to be printed in gold, because it was in that year that the singlemost important invention in the whole transportation industry was announced: the Westinghouse Air Brake, a device that stopped the dreadful loss of lives of employees and passengers, and made railroad travel the safest means of travel to this day. George Westinghouse was a young Union Navy assistant engineer, just back from the Civil War. He had already invented the rotary engine and a rerailing frog for trains when he witnessed a head-on collision near Schenectady, New York. He was only twenty-four years old when he was given permission to demonstrate his new "atmospheric brake" on Pennsylvania Railroad's No. 13, a very handsome 4-4-0. He put an air pump and tank on the engine and ran an air line from car to car, leading to a set of piston-operated brakes on each car. The idea was that when the engineer opened a valve, compressed air would set the brakes. Few people thought it would work.

The test train, on its way to Steubenville, Ohio, clanked out of Grant's Hill Tunnel in Pittsburgh, but right there on the tracks ahead of it was a team of horses and a loaded wagon. For the first time the

Jan Gleysteen

engineer touched the new lever. He pulled it all the way for an emergency stop. The train slid to a stop only four feet from the terrified horses. Never before had such a sudden stop been possible. The dramatic moment was recounted all over the United States, and the Westinghouse Air Brakes gained immediate acceptance. Rumors persist that George Westinghouse arranged for the farmer to be on the crossing. In that case he also deserves credit for a Madison Avenue approach to selling his idea.

The first air brake had one shortcoming: if a train broke in two, the brakes wouldn't work. So Westinghouse reversed the system and put pressure in the lines to keep the brakes off. Should the pressure go down due to a leak or break, the brakes would set automatically.

George Westinghouse continued to create new inventions. He registered 361 patents in all, or one for every six weeks of his working years. But his fortune, which enabled him to set up more than sixty companies, came from the air brake. In 1955, forty-one years after his death, George Westinghouse was elected to the Hall of Fame for Great Americans.

As the 19th century came to a close, new improvements and services followed each other in rapid succession. The camelback locomotive was born of necessity on the Eastern railroads. In the 1880's the northeastern Pennsylvania coal fields yielded anthracite which burned with great difficulty in engines designed for soft-coal use. In answer to this problem, the designers came up with engines with increasingly larger fire grates, extending well beyond the rear set of drivers. In 1880 the general manager of the Philadelphia and

Reading, John E. Wootten, took out patents on an engine with an extremely wide and shallow firebox, placed above the driving wheels. Since a conventional cab on top of all this would not clear structures along the right-of-way, Wootten moved the cab forward to straddle the boiler, dividing the cab in two narrow compartments. The first camelback was given the classification 4-4-0 w (w stands for Wootten).

The camelbacks were at first sharply criticized, not so much on performance, but because locomotives "just don't look like that." But they were practical and eventually fifty railroads in the United States and Mexico used them in sizes ranging from small 0-4-0's to mammoth 0-8-8-0 Mallets. The camelbacks were a colorful lot, but not always popular with the personnel. The cab was just two feet wide, full of gauges scattered on the boiler, and located right above the driving rods. If an engine threw a rod right under the engineer's feet, he didn't live to report it. The fireman rode the tail, feeding the fire without a view of the tracks ahead, and without the possibility of communication with the engineer. Even so this exotic breed served the railroads of the hard-coal region well for nearly seventy years.

While the railroads provided the industrial East with a tight network of rails that took care of the lion's share of shipping, the cattlemen of the great Southwest still drove their mammoth herds to market over the Chisholm Trail. At Abilene, Kansas, the Longhorns were loaded in the cars of the Kansas Pacific, now Union Pacific, for the remainder of their trip to Chicago. The first cattle trains probably left from Abilene in 1867. Between 1875 and 1885 the Santa Fe shipped more than 3,000 carloads of cattle a year, from the trail ending at Dodge City. The Rock Island began to receive its share of the business at Caldwell, Kansas, in September, 1887. Photographs of smoke-belching 4-4-0's pulling cattle cars abound in every historical collection.

The long, hot, dusty drive from the grazing grounds of eastern Texas, across the Red River Valley, and through Oklahoma meant lots of hard work for the cowboys. When they had finally delivered the herds to the railheads, they were ready to celebrate in style. The rail towns were well equipped for them with a large selection of saloons, gambling joints, and dance halls. Newton, Kansas, became known as "shootin' Newton" because nine men died there in duels on a single boisterous night.

In 1889 the Pennsy designed and developed the famous Belpaire Boiler and tried it out on eight-wheeler 1321. The purpose of the design was to create a boiler top to conform more nearly to, and run parallel with, the crown sheet beneath. Thus each staybolt would be at right angles with both surfaces. The design was very successful and was adopted by many other roads. The exceptions were roads with poor water, where the Belpaire boiler afforded too good a hold for scale.

The progressive Pennsylvania line scored another first in 1892 when the Pennsylvania Limited was the first train in the United States to be lighted by electricity. The headlight on the class D10a type still looks for all practical purposes like a conventional oil light. Two other lines that placed electric lights on 4-4-0's at an early date were the Kansas City Southern and the Texas and Pacific around 1894.

The cab-forwards described at the beginning of this chapter could only exist as oil burners. Locomotive fuel oil had been successfully used in Russia since 1874, and sixty engines of the English Great Eastern were delivered as oil burners in 1886. In 1881 the Grant Locomotive Works seems to have built a naptha-burning 4-4-0 for the New York Heat, Light, and Power Company, but the "C. Holland" was a costly and dangerous failure that was scrapped after only a few runs.

Out across the continent, in the Western states, coal was imported from Australia at $7.50 a ton. So four years later, in 1885, the master mechanic of the Southern Pacific at Los Angeles succeeded in converting a Schenectady-built 4-4-0 into a very efficient oil burner. It was retired in 1919 after thirty-eight years of faithful service. The Union Oil Company of California states that from the first few hundred barrels of oil used by locomotives in 1884, the consumption of oil on steam locomotives had grown to 70,094,416 barrels in 1927, as supplied by their company alone.

Not all the experiments turned out to be of practical value. Two noteworthy failures were the Fontaine engines and Holman's absurdity. Fontaine's engine was similar to the friction toys of our days. Eugene Fontaine of Detroit arranged with the Grant Locomotive Works to have three locomotives built. Engine No. 1 proved to be deficient, engine No. 2 was never completed, and the 4-4-0 No. 3 was outshopped by Grant in September, 1881. The driving wheels of this 4-4-0 were not connected to the cylinders, but the front driver was moved by a larger diameter driver-flywheel located directly above it. This, Fontaine thought, would make a seventy-inch driver do the work of an engine with ninety-inch drivers. Fontaine forgot that while a two-pulley block and tackle will allow a man to lift twice as much weight as he can with a single pulley, he must pull the rope twice as far to do it. The Toledo Commercial Telegram reported later:

"The two Fontaine engines constructed a few years ago will be remembered by all railroad men, one of the engines with a freight train attached having made 15 miles in 10 minutes or 90 miles an hour, on the old Canada Southern track between this city and Monroe, Michigan. The two engines were constructed at a cost of $45,000, including the expenses of the tests. They were tried on several roads only to demonstrate the mechanical axiom that what is gained in speed is lost in power. A greater speed than 60 miles an hour is not considered an advantage and the saving in fuel promised in this engine was not proved. The engines were tried on the Hudson River, the Canada Southern, and the Oxford & Port Austin railroads and Saturday the closing scene in their history occurred by their sale for $2,700.00 to the Lake Erie & Western Railroad. This road will place them in the shop where they will be reduced to the ordinary style of locomotive and the Fontaine engine will live only in memory."

While Fontaine's engine had some merit, the Holman absurdity was a classic example of how not to go about improving an engine. The first Holman engine was a rebuilt 4-4-0 of the Minneapolis, St. Paul and Sault Ste. Marie line put on the track in 1894. The second one was actually built new by Baldwin in 1897. The locomotives were of conventional design but had small drivers, each of which rested on two smaller wheels, which in turn drove six still smaller wheels that touched the track. This nightmare was eventually sold to the South Jersey Railroad, where she spent most of her life in the shops on down time. When she did run she rocked like a canoe in mid-ocean and her crew was plenty scared. She was soon rebuilt into a conventional 4-4-0.

CHAPTER FOUR

Through Fire and Frost

One of the most unusual actions in modern American locomotive history was the preparation in 1954, by the Baldwin Locomotive Works, of a formal estimate of the cost of reproducing an early American type, in connection with the litigation for the recovery of such a locomotive or the equivalent value thereof.

The history leading to this unusual action was this. On October 18, 1882, the Baldwin Locomotive Works delivered a standard gauge 4-4-0 to the Morgan, Louisiana and Texas Railway and Steamship Company. She was delivered in time to contribute her share to the construction of the second transcontinental route, completed in 1885 as part of the Southern Pacific System. The Southern Pacific later took over all the subsidiary lines and equipment and M.L.T. No. 44 became S.P. 544.

In 1901 the 544 was assigned to a branch line operating out of Lafayette, Louisiana, and in 1914 the engine was sold to the Meeker Sugar Refinery for switching service. In their weed-grown yards she was discovered quite by accident, in the summer of 1948, by Mr. A. E. LaSalle, president of the American Railroad Equipment Association. After a year of negotiations, necessitated by having to find a small suitable diesel for replacement, Mr. LaSalle became the lucky owner of old 44, and began restoring it right at the Meeker factory yard. After a complete overhaul and nearly finished restoration, No. 44 was steamed up twice and operated. The tender was lettered Hermitage Plantation R.R., the name of her proposed future home. These plans were changed, however, and she was instead loaded up and moved to the Oaklawn Manor Plantation, home of Clyde Barbour, where she found a beautiful setting of live oaks and Spanish moss to match her glory.

Unfortunately, Oaklawn Manor became involved in a family litigation, and in the skirmish old 44 was dis-

mantled one night and removed from the property. The engine had been stolen!

In the lawsuit that followed the difficult thing to establish was the value of such a relic. It was at this point that Baldwin was called upon to produce a complete estimate of the cost of reproducing one of their own earlier products. The price Baldwin quoted in 1954 to reproduce exactly an 1882 engine was $121,330. The lawsuit was finally settled by the delivery of the narrow-gauge Mogul "Albert" to Mr. LaSalle, who likewise restored it to mint condition.

No. 44's destruction has never really been proven, but it seems very likely. Her greatest honor came belatedly. In 1959 the Smithsonian Institute requested her purchase and removal to Washington, D.C. They had known nothing about the tragedy.

Following is only one example, and a very black one indeed, of how the dependable American could also be depended on to find itself in unusual situations. The following event took place in my home state of Pennsylvania nearly one hundred years ago.

Late in the evening of August 17, 1869, a small mixed train, consisting of two passenger cars and six wooden two-barrel oil cars (similar to the one preserved at Titusville, Pennsylvania), and a boxcar with horses and their keepers, left Maysville Summit to travel a fourteen-mile downgrade stretch of the Buffalo, Corry & Pittsburgh Railroad across the Pennsylvania-New York state boundary. Two miles out of town the crew noticed that one of the oil cars was on fire. They quickly stopped the train and set the brakes on the burning oil cars—all six were aflame by that time. They pulled the pin between the boxcar and tank number 1, and moved the engine ahead, intent on saving at least this one car and the engine itself. Imagine the horror of the crew when they discovered that the brakes of the blazing oil cars had failed, and thanks to the favorable grade, the cars were rapidly bearing down on them. Engineer Duff Brown and his fireman worked feverishly to maintain a gap between them and this hell on wheels fed by 50,000 gallons of oil. At a speed never before believed possible, they approached Brocton, New York, whistle screaming. Thanks to the presence of mind of the switch tender at Brocton, a collision with the Cincinnati Express on the Lake Shore Line was averted, and the switches were set to send the locomotive and boxcar whizzing past the depot, the blazing oil cars still close on their heels, lighting the night sky with a streak of flame a hundred feet long.

But the race had been won. On the upgrade beyond Brocton the oil cars lost momentum, and for the next three hours burned brightly on the Lake Shore siding. The engineer and his fireman were both exhausted and suffering from shock after covering the sixteen miles between Summit and the siding in twelve minutes at a speed of eighty miles per hour. The horsemen in the car behind were found unconscious but alive.

This race from a fire was followed by a race to a fire in which Lou Hawk's dramatic run of 186 miles in 150 minutes became a legend. This was on the night of the great Chicago fire in 1871. Lou came to the rescue with the 4-4-0 "Major Nolton," No. 93 on the Chicago & Alton, pulling a trainload of fire-fighting equipment sent up from Bloomington.

Two decades later, in September, 1894, engineer James Root used his 4-4-0 and train, the Duluth Limited of the St. Paul and Duluth R.R., to rescue the citizens of Hinkley, Minnesota, who were trapped in a raging forest fire. He kept running his train through the flames on mercy missions even though his clothes were burning. Root's fireman, himself hidden in the tank, threw buckets of water on him. Jimmy Root picked up as many people as he could and brought his train through the flames to a halt on the causeway along Skunk Lake, actually a swamp. Here the badly burnt survivors and crew crouched in the water while the train was reduced to ashes before their very eyes. Jim Root, unconscious when the grateful people laid him in the water, lived to tell the story and should be remembered as one of the greatest heroes ever to pilot a 4-4-0.

While some Americans performed well in the heat, others showed their superiority in the other extreme of temperature. Numerous pictures survive showing eight Central Pacific engines pushing a pilot plow up Donner Pass to keep the Overland Route open in the winter of 1870. Because snowdrifts sometimes reached thirty feet high, the railroad eventually covered about forty miles of this route with a wooden snow shed, causing one engineer to remark: "I have served many a line

from coast to coast but this is the first time I have done my railroading in a barn."

Snow was often a hindrance, but ice could be of help. The Susquehanna River was not bridged until 1866, but between January 15 and February 24, 1852, a total of 1,378 cars of mail, passengers, and freight crossed the frozen river. The caption on a contemporary print reports: "The cars were nearly all eight-wheel cars and were all passed without the slightest injury to any person or property. The amount of tonnage crossed was about 10,000 tons of which 4,000 was merchandise." The print shows that the locomotives did not venture onto the ice, but pulled cuts of two or three cars across with a long cable. While this is probably the earliest occurrence of trains on the river, it is by no means the only one. And in all the subsequent reports the locomotive went along on the ice.

In 1880 the Canadians laid a temporary line across the deeply frozen St. Lawrence between Hochelago and Longueil. In the hard winter of 1882 the Northern Pacific laid rails across the Missouri between Mandan and Brunswick. The pictures show mixed trains making the icy run behind diamond-stacked 4-4-0's. In the summertime the crossing here took place with ferries. Laying tracks across frozen lakes or rivers was much easier for the already portable logging railroads. A few 4-4-0's did serve the logging interests in northern Michigan. An old newspaper from those parts includes a photo of a narrow-gauge 4-4-0, decorated with evergreen and deer antlers, hauling a long string of pine logs over the ice for the Cody and Moore R.R. near Lake City, Michigan, during the Christmas season of 1885.

A roadbed of ice, treacherous though it sounds, was often more secure than some of the permanent right-of-ways. In some swampy areas, notably in the Louisiana bayous, companies sometimes felled a few trees, laid the logs end to end, and covered them crosswise in corduroy fashion (all or not covered with earth), and hoped for the best. Washouts and spreading track were common. In March, 1885, Texas & Pacific engine 642 rolled through the spring rain, bound for Texarkana. Crossing Village Creek, the engine broke through the small wooden trestle and disappeared in the swirling waters, followed by the mail and baggage cars. Engineer Lyman S. Roach survived. Crippled from the wreck, he quit railroading. His brother-in-law J. G. Habeck, the fireman, was found dead three miles downstream. The cars were salvaged in due time, and the bridge was repaired. But the old 4-4-0 is still entombed in the quicksands of Village Creek. In 1936 a section of the stack came up. The rest of the engine remains buried under the present heavier bridge abutments erected in the late 1920's, a stalwart pioneer in an unmarked grave.

One sturdy eight-wheeler, the "Milwaukee" of the old Welland Railway in Ontario, helped repel the only invasion of Canada attempted since the war of 1812. Hundreds of Irish soldiers, on their own with the ending of the Civil War, formed the Fenian Society, a group bent on separating Ireland from the British Empire. Armed and well organized they crossed the Niagara River and advanced on Port Colborne in June, 1866. John Flack, a telegrapher on the Welland Railway, tapped out the news over his wires, then joined the volunteers as the "Milwaukee" readied a train of men and supplies to drive the Fenians back in a triumphal run out of St. Catherines. Trains proved their worth in war and peace.

After World War II the famous Friendship Trains were assembled, bound for New York with hundreds of tons of food for the hungry people of Europe. But the Friendship Trains had a historic counterpart.

In 1874 a grasshopper plague devastated the Kansas plains around Wichita and Sedgwick, and this disaster was followed by a long dry summer. In the East, in the Ohio Valley, crops had never been better. When news of the conditions in Kansas reached them, they responded promptly: "Let's send in a trainful. Let's all pitch in to fill the empty cars and give thanks to God that it isn't us, and that we can share." Because of this generous reaction from along the Ohio, the people of Sedgwick and Wichita felt encouraged to try again.

A decade passed and in 1884 the Ohio River went on a rampage tearing up farms and orchards and carrying away barns and livestock. When this news reached Kansas, it was their turn to say: "Let's send in a trainful." A sketch in "Harper's Weekly" shows the thirty-one highly decorated cars of the "Corn Train" on a siding in Wichita, Kansas, behind an eight-wheeler equal to the task.

Sometimes engines ran away or were used to run away with. In 1908 a Chicago, Bluffton, and Cincinnati R.R. engine ran away at Huntingdon, Indiana, and finally worked itself into a candy store.

On February 21, 1883, five convicts escaped from Sing-Sing, hijacked New York Central's American No. 89, and forced engineer Dan Cassin to run her at full speed. Two of the escapees were recaptured, one was killed, and two vanished.

Can you imagine an electric railway buying steam locomotives? The Pacific Electric used a tall-stacked twin-dome eight-wheeler between 1911 and 1924. The engine was marked Pacific Electric 1500, and from the looks of the tender it was probably an oil burner. But the real sight to see was in Milwaukee, Oregon, where in 1940 an American-type locomotive was assigned as a head end helper engine on the southbound Southern Pacific freights. The line is upgrade toward Woodburn for a distance of about thirty miles. Just close your eyes and try to imagine an American leading a massive cab-in-front articulated, like David bringing in Goliath!

CHAPTER FIVE

Whirling Wheels

On the evening of May 31, 1876, the famous actor, Lawrence Barrett, was winding up his New York performance at Broadway's Booth Theatre. His successful appearance in New York was arranged and managed by the impressario, Henry C. Jarrett of Jarrett and Palmer, owners of the Booth Theatre. Now Lawrence Barrett and his colleagues, Frederick Thorne and C. B. Bishop, were also booked to appear in Shakespeare's "Henry V" at the McCullough Theatre in San Francisco on Monday, June 5. The fastest scheduled service between New York and San Francisco in 1876 required seven days, with changes of trains and stations in Chicago and Omaha.

It is not known now whether the idea of making a fast run across the continent originated with the actor or his impressario, but an agreement with the railroads was made to operate a through train on a tentative schedule of eighty-four hours for the occasion. This "Lightning Train" would be a fulfillment of one of Jules Verne's fantasies never before thought possible, and the promotional value of being on a train that ran a week's distance in $3\frac{1}{2}$ days was not lost on the actors.

The trip, now nearly a century past, is well documented because the newspapers, notably the "New York Herald," took a very active interest in the performance. They gave the story front-page coverage and helped finance the stunt. The New York Post Office also capitalized on the occasion to forward their mail west at a record pace.

While Lawrence Barrett collected his belongings and made his last appearance on the Broadway stage, a four-year-old class C 4-4-0, No. 573 of the Pennsylvania Railroad, was moved from Pittsburgh to Jersey City. The "Samuel J. Tilden" was handpicked from the roster for its excellent service record. It was equipped with copper tubes and flexible hose for oiling en route. This was possibly another first in railroading. The train itself consisted of three cars—a baggage car, a combine,

and a Pullman. The baggage car was adapted to carry some 4,000 pounds of reserve coal and 1,600 extra gallons of water, besides the scenery and stage props. The whole train was lettered in gold on red: Jarrett's and Palmer's Special Transcontinental Express.

Copies of the June 1 "New York Herald" were printed and delivered to the baggage car in loose sheets, to be assembled en route for delivery in Chicago that same day, another unprecedented feat.

The train left New York at 12:40 a.m., June 1, and passed West Philadelphia at 2:40 a.m. ("the brilliantly lighted buildings made a magnificent night scene"). The special passed through Harrisburg, Pennsylvania, at 5:18 a.m. ("3,000 people were grouped on the platforms"). The train arrived in Pittsburgh at 10:39, two minutes ahead of schedule, and car inspectors declared the train in good condition. From Pittsburgh to Chicago thousands of people lined the right-of-way to greet the train and to wish it good speed on the remainder of the trip. From Chicago to Boone, Iowa, a night section of the run, citizens had lighted bonfires at practically every crossing. And so it went from one state into the next.

The most exciting part of the trip was near the end, when the train ate up the 879 miles between Ogden, Utah, and the Pacific Coast in 23 hours and 45 minutes. Under the hand of Hank Small at the driver's side, Central Pacific's 4-4-0 "Black Fox" averaged thirty-seven miles per hour, including sixteen stops, on this most trying portion of the run through the Sierras. The train arrived in San Francisco on Sunday, June 4, at 9:39 a.m., eighty-four hours and seven minutes after leaving New York City, now 3,313.5 miles behind them. The best performance of the whole run was made by the Pennsylvania engine, which maintained an average speed of 43.5 miles on the first lap of this historic trip.

This run, never to be repeated, caught the fancy of the public, who responded with an enthusiasm not witnessed again until Lindbergh's flight across the Atlantic. There had been a few speed runs before, but none before or since over such a distance. Possibly the earliest speed run took place in 1848 somewhere between Albany and Buffalo, New York, with a six-foot-drivered 4-4-0. The engine was Auburn and Syracuse Railroad's locomotive "Howe" which was delivered in August, 1848, by Rogers, Ketchum, and Grosvenor. Shortly thereafter it left Syracuse with a train of four coaches and one baggage car with William Delano as engineer and Thomas Hooper as fireman. Guests on the engine were William's brother, Howard, and Cyrus Dennis, one of the railroad officials. This may have been their first train ride. To see how fast the "Howe" could run, the engineer opened her up till she hit the unheard-of speed of sixty miles per hour. Sixteen miles west of Syracuse the entire train left the rails. The engineer and fireman were killed, Howard Delano was injured, and Mr. Dennis disfigured for life from the escaping steam.

The Auburn and Syracuse later became a part of the New York Central System, which was a consolidation of twelve independent roads prior to 1856. Quite a few impressive records were made on the Central. On July 4, 1875, the New York Central in conjunction with the city newspapers began operating a Sunday Edition Special to deliver the news to Niagara Falls, 470 miles away, in eleven hours. No 110, a McQueen-built 4-4-0, was assigned to run on the division between Syracuse and Buffalo. Once hauling three cars she left Syracuse thirty minutes late and arrived in Buffalo five minutes ahead of schedule. That was really clipping off the miles.

In 1869 the New York Central merged with the Hudson River Railroad. With the Hudson River Railroad came a man of exceptional ability: William Buchanan, their master mechanic for the past ten years. It can safely be said that Buchanan developed the eight-wheeler to its peak of perfection during his reign as motive power superintendent of the Central. His 4-4-0's made the successful operation of the Empire State Express possible, after test runs had demonstrated that an average speed of 61.4 miles per hour could consistently be maintained between New York and Buffalo.

The world-famous 999 was a Buchanan creation delivered from the West Albany Shops in 1893. After trial runs it was assigned to the Empire State Express. Although the 999 was no better than any other Buchanan type, her seven-foot plus drivers gave her an amazing speed. On May 10, 1893, Charlie Hogan, who regularly handled the 999 on the almost gradeless division between Syracuse and Buffalo, was instructed to really let her roll and run the 999 faster than any engine in the world. Between Batavia and Buffalo Charlie coaxed the beauty up to the world record of 112½ mph. Back in the buffet car the reporters and officials held their stopwatches and verified a speed no human had ever experienced. A mile clicked by in 40 seconds, then in 38, and finally a mile was covered in 31.2 seconds. No train or any other man-made vehicle had ever moved so fast. Charlie Hogan in his cab looked out over the straight track ahead as the tall drivers under him churned at more than 440 rounds per minute. The 999's record was unsurpassed for several decades.

With the name Empire State Express in Spencerian script lettered on her tender, the 999 drew awestruck admiration during the rest of the year as she was exhibited at the World's Columbian Exposition in Chicago. In 1901 she was honored on a commemorative two-cent stamp in connection with the Pan-American Exposition in Buffalo.

In sustained high-speed passenger service the 999 was not equal to some other Buchanan 4-4-0's, specifically No. 870, which turned in many notable speed records over greater distances. But the 999 still lives on. In 1899 her drivers were reduced to seventy inches. She was exhibited at three more fairs, for two years each. Finally in 1962 she became the property of the Chicago Museum of Science and Industry. She arrived in Chicago coupled tailfirst to a diesel, a situa-

23

tion likely to cause the great master mechanic to shudder in his grave.

The feats of the 999 created a favorable image for the New York Central and gained the line a lot of business on their New York-Chicago Express. Not to be left behind, the Pennsylvania took up the challenge and responded with their famous D16 class 4-4-0's, which some critics acclaim to be the most beautiful modern engines of this wheel arrangement. Although the speed capabilities of the D16's never achieved the publicity of N.Y.C.'s 999, they were nevertheless top-notch speedsters. One example is a record on the 903, which in the late 90's covered the twelve miles between Metuchen and Rahway, New Jersey, in eight minutes, at 102 miles per hour. Engines on the Pennsy's high-speed seashore line frequently maintained a pace of eighty miles per hour over long stretches. There were 429 of these D16's on the Pennsylvania Railroad, outnumbering by a small margin of four the famous K4 Pacifics. In 1910, when New York City required the use of electric locomotives within the city limits, the Pennsylvania made extensive tests over a special section of track near Franklinville, New Jersey, which was equipped with eighty specially designed recording ties. As a result the P.R.R. built the DD1 electrics, which were actually like two Americans back to back. It permitted in electric locomotives the riding qualities long associated with the D16. One of the famous D16's, No. 1223, is preserved and displayed at the Strasburg Rail Road in eastern Pennsylvania.

The same year the 999 set its record, the 4-4-0 locomotive "Nancy Hanks" managed to clip some three hours off the daily Atlanta-Savannah run over the Central of Georgia and earned for its owners the coveted title, "Fastest Railroad in the South." Even British rail circles took notice of its schedule. But after four months, "Nancy" was bridled, her speed being greater than the condition of rolling stock and roadbed could endure. It must be remembered that normal train speeds in the United States in those days were quite slow. Using a minimum speed of forty miles on a run of at least forty miles in length as the standard for a fast train, E. Foxwell and T. C. Farrar in 1898 concluded that fast trains in the States served only 13,956 miles of regularly scheduled runs compared to nearly five times that many for Great Britain.

In 1884 the New Haven inaugurated one of the fastest and most luxurious trains of all times. Officially named the New England Limited, it was better known as the White Train or the Ghost Train. Consisting of seven cars painted from buffer to buffer in creamy white with delicate gold striping, the White Train was pulled by a high-stepping 4-4-0 (No. 167 or No. 129) with twin headlights and a large white Maltese Cross on the tender. At each terminal the coal was whitewashed to harmonize with the idea, and the crew wore white jackets and caps. The regular engineer, Gene Potter, frequently ran his train at 80 mph and better through the Connecticut meadows. In 1895 the White Train was discontinued, but it passed into history as one of the most beautiful consists ever to run behind a 4-4-0.

On September 11, 1901, a camelback 4-4-0 on the Lackawanna, with John Draney at the throttle, was rushed from New York to Buffalo to deliver Dr. Edward C. Janeway to the bedside of President McKinley, who had been shot by an anarchist. The Lackawanna was selected, since the Delaware, Lackawanna, and Western was fifteen miles shorter than the New York Central. Draney in the cab of No. 936 made the 396-mile run in 405 minutes, reaching at one point a top speed of 115 miles per hour, three miles over the world record. But since the claim for this speed was not verified, it was never made an official record.

Not all the speed running took place on passenger trains. The fast mail became an American legend, too. American railroads have been carrying mail since 1831. The South Carolina Rail Road began doing so. The first true mail car was a converted baggage car on the Hannibal and St. Joseph Railroad in Missouri. It made its inaugural run on July 28, 1862, carrying mail destined for the pony express. A replica of this car is now in existence.

The first Railway Post Office in which mail, picked up en route, was sorted by R.P.O. clerks began service two years later between Chicago and Clinton, Iowa, on the Chicago and North Western Railroad. In 1871 Tommy Holmes, a nineteen-year-old engineer, won a lucrative mail contract on the Chicago-Omaha run for the Rock Island, using the famous silver engine "America" to beat the competition. In turn the Burlington won the contract for carrying the transcontinental mails between Chicago and Council Bluffs, inaugurating their fast mail in May, 1884. The mail contract was highly prized and jealously guarded. Daring but capable engineers were chosen to run engines tuned to perfection. The Lake Shore and Michigan Southern groomed high-stepping 4-4-0, No. 317, to pull a train of gleaming white and gold postal cars. The train covered the New York-Chicago trip in twenty-four hours. Even so, the train was taken off in ten months because it netted more prestige than revenue.

The romance of a swift 4-4-0 racing toward her destination with four or five Railway Post Offices, smoke streaming from her diamond stack—the Fast Mail in all her glory—will never be equaled by the boxy mail trucks of our time.

CHAPTER SIX

Moments of Glory

A locomotive and three boxcars were lifted from under the very noses of the Confederate soldiers in the early morning of April 12, 1862. The conductor of the train had just started on his breakfast at Big Shanty, Georgia, now called Kennesaw, when he saw his train depart without him. He chased it on foot, not knowing at that time that he was about to play a major part in the most exciting spy story of the Civil War.

In the spring of 1862 the Confederate front extended roughly between Memphis, Tennessee, and Virginia's northern counties. The Western and Atlantic Railroad between Chattanooga and Atlanta served as an important link to the front lines north of Chattanooga. Union generals felt that if they could cripple this source of men and supplies, or even sever it temporarily, they might end, or at least greatly shorten, the slaughter of brothers and sons that had begun only a year before.

Assigned to execute this bold plan was a thirty-three-year-old Union secret agent, James J. Andrews of Flemingsburg, Kentucky. During the first week of April, Andrews and nineteen Union soldiers, all in civilian clothes, worked their way into Georgia. At Marietta they all bought tickets to different points and early in the morning boarded a northbound mixed train pulled by the W. & A.R.R. locomotive, "General." Around 6:00 a.m. the train stopped at Big Shanty, Georgia, ten miles up the line, where a trainman sang out, "Big Shanty, twenty minutes off for breakfast!" While tired and hungry passengers and crew filed into the dining room of the Lacy Hotel, Andrews and his men remained aboard the train. Then, unnoticed by the armed guard, and in full sight of the 3,000-man Confederate Camp McDonald, they uncoupled the "General" and three boxcars from the rest of the train. Suddenly the quiet of the morning was shattered by the hiss of steam, spinning drivers, and a violent huff of

smoke. The short train shot forward, picked up speed, and was soon out of sight.

Inside the hotel, conductor William A. Fuller looked up in disbelief. Shouting to the other railroad men, "Someone who has no right to do so has gone off with our train," he dashed outside just in time to see the last car disappear. With no idea who might have stolen the train, Fuller, accompanied by engineer Jeff Cain and shop foreman Anthony Murphy, ran down the tracks in pursuit. Two miles north at Moon station they found a handcar. Taking turns, two running behind and one resting, they continued the race. The next few miles were a downhill stretch known as the big grade to the Shanties. They made good time to Etowah, where they commandeered the "Yonah," an old switcher of the Cooper Iron Works.

Starting afoot from Big Shanty, Fuller had little hope of catching his train. Now aboard the "Yonah" he became more optimistic. And, unbeknown to both parties, events were taking place at Kingston fifteen miles ahead, that would further close the gap between the pursuers and the pursued.

As they sped along in the stolen "General," Andrews and his raiders met little opposition. Periodically they stopped to cut telegraph wires and to place obstacles on the track. But then, as they steamed into the important junction town of Kingston, they found the road ahead blocked by three southbound freights. An agonizing hour ticked by as the raiders waited. All except Andrews and three men in the cab were hidden in the boxcars, and all feared that they would be discovered during the long wait.

The railroad officials at Kingston eyed Andrews and the "General" suspiciously until Andrews convinced them that in reality he was a Confederate officer on a special mission. He explained that it was of the greatest importance that his train, loaded with ammunition for

General Beauregard, arrive promptly in Chattanooga. For good measure Andrews gave an inspiring and passionate speech on Southern patriotism. No one dared to question his authority after that, and when the last of the southbound trains were switched to the sidings, the "General" and its crew sped on.

And just in time, for only minutes later the "Yonah," with Fuller, Cain, and Murphy, raced into Kingston to find that the raiders had just left. Hearing the station agent's tale, it now dawned on Fuller that the men on his train were really Yankee spies bent on the destruction of the Western and Atlantic.

Taking the locomotive "William R. Smith" from the last southbound freight, Fuller continued the chase. Three miles ahead they screeched to a halt, narrowly avoiding a stretch of damaged track. The sabotaged section prevented them from going any further, but they continued on foot for about two miles where they hailed still another southbound freight pulled by the locomotive "Texas." Fuller persuaded the engineer to back up to Adairsville, where the train could be dropped. From Adairsville the chase began in earnest as now two locomotives, the "Texas" going in reverse, sped over the light iron at nearly sixty miles per hour. Both engines were powerful for their time, each with 140 pounds of steam and five-foot drivers. One year younger and every bit the equal of the "General," the "Texas" began to narrow the gap between it and the Northern spies. Then, rounding a curve two miles north of Calhoun, it swept in sight of the fugitives. The "General" was stopped and a group of men behind it were prying up rail. The sight of the "Texas" sent the men scurrying aboard the "General," but Andrews realized that the contest had become too close for him to achieve anything more than delaying tactics. No doubt their main concern now was how to save their own skins. In desperation, they twice reversed the drivers on the "General," sending off two of the three boxcars, hoping the "Texas" would be wrecked by a collision. It didn't work. Engineer Beckley on the "Texas" skillfully caught the cars and shoved them into a siding on the fly.

Under full steam the "General" raced through Dalton, Georgia, the "Texas" right behind slowing down only long enough to drop off a telegraph operator to send a message to Chattanooga. North of Dalton both engines rushed into Tunnel Hill. Only lack of time prevented Andrews' raiders from preparing a cruel surprise for the "Texas" in the darkness of the tunnel. The "Texas" backed blindly into it, hot on the heels of the stolen American and its cabful of Union men.

Andrews finally left his remaining boxcar, drenched with coal oil, in the covered bridge across the Chicka-manga. But a steady rain was against Andrews and the bridge did not burn.

Finally near Ringgold, Georgia, the last of the wood had gone into the fire, and no more water showed on the gauge. The "General" slowed down to twenty-five miles per hour, then twenty, fifteen. Cavalry men were advancing quickly from the north. "Stop her, Knight! It's every man for himself now." Andrews had given his last order. Each raider scattered in the brush along the railroad. Two miles north at the crest of a grade the "General" stopped. The daring raid that was intended to shorten the war had failed. The eighty-seven mile, eight-hour chase was over when the "Texas" drew up behind the deserted "General."

Confederate cavalry combed all northern Georgia in search of the "engine thieves," and within a week had captured all of them. In June, 1862, Andrews, who had previously stated, "I'll succeed in this, or I'll leave my bones in Dixie," and seven of the raiders, were publicly hanged in Atlanta. Also condemned to die, eight others escaped from the Atlanta prison. The remaining fourteen were paroled in 1863. The Union felt a deep debt to the men who had started the chase and the Confederacy to those who finished it. The Union men were awarded Congressional Medals of Honor, and the Confederates were commended by the governor of Alabama.

The hero of this story, the locomotive "General," is still in existence. Still spry and very much alive at the age of 110, she is probably the best known American-type locomotive in the world.

The "General" was a 4-4-0 built by Rogers, Ketchum, and Grosvenor of Paterson, New Jersey. It was bought by the Western and Atlantic Railroad in 1855 for $8,850. The eight-hour flight north in the hands of Andrews' raiders left it unharmed. It was picked up by the "Texas" at the end of the chase and towed back to Ringgold. From there it was returned to Atlanta for checkup.

The following two years were very uneventful for the "General," but in July, 1864, during the battle of Kennesaw Mountain the engine helped to move supplies in and to transport wounded out. Its most perilous moment came during the final days of the siege of Atlanta. The "General" and four or five other locomotives were left in Atlanta in an attempt to move eighty-one cars of ammunition to safety. But time had run out and on the night of September 1, 1864, retreating members of the Georgia militia set fuses to the train. Explosions rocked the entire eastern section of Atlanta as all the cars, two of the engines, and a nearby steel mill went up in one of the most spectacular displays of foolishness of the war. Parts of three loco-

motives survived the holocaust. One, badly battered but still identifiable, was the "General."

In 1871 the "General" was rebuilt and its appearance changed to look very much as it does today. Later in that decade it was converted to a coal burner and given a diamond stack. It last saw active service in March, 1886, near Kennesaw, close to where it had been stolen twenty-four years earlier. In 1891 the "General" was taken from a weed-grown siding at Vinnings Station, Georgia, to the L. & N. shops at Nashville, where it was restored to its original appearance and then placed on exhibit in the Union Station of Chattanooga.

In 1961 the "General" was awakened from its long rest and taken to Louisville, Kentucky, to be reconditioned to run again under its own power.

For some eight months following its removal from Chattanooga, the "General" underwent a thorough going-over in the shops of the L. & N. at Louisville. There it was completely dismantled and every part given a minute examination. Amazingly enough, despite its age of 107, it was in good repair.

The only major items needing replacement were a new set of flues in the boiler, new axles and new tires for the drivers. Air brakes also were added in order to comply with Interstate Commerce Commission regulations.

Originally a wood burner, later a coal burner, the "General" is now an oil burner, but oil merely furnishes the heat to produce the steam. Today, in the diesel age, the L. & N. has no water tanks along the line, so while on tour, local fire departments supply the "General's" water requirements.

The "General" toured extensively during the 1964-65 Civil War Centennial and will probably return to Chattanooga.

The "Texas," also a 4-4-0 type, was built by Danforth & Cooke, also of Paterson, New Jersey, at a cost of $9,050, and was placed in service on the W. & A.R.R. in September, 1856. When the war ended it was located in Virginia and returned to its owners. It was still running in 1903, but in 1907, worn and rusty, it was sent to Atlanta to be scrapped. Public opinion demanded that it be preserved and in 1911 the city of Atlanta accepted the engine and put it on display in Grant Park.

In 1927 it was moved to the basement of the Cyclorama where it can be seen today. In the 1930's it was carefully restored.

The "William B. Smith" was built by Norris & Co., Philadelphia. Regularly in freight service on the Rome Railroad, it was substituting for the passenger engine on the day of the chase. During the latter part of the war it was loaned to the South Western & Muscogee Railroad of Columbus, Georgia, where it was damaged beyond repair, April 16, 1865, during a raid by Wilson's cavalry.

The locomotive "Yonah," used between Etowah and Kingston, was not a 4-4-0. Built in 1849, it was later used as a stationary boiler and scrapped around 1870.

Partly because the Great Locomotive Chase ended as a failure, the war between the states continued for another three years. And when the armistice finally came, hundreds of miles of railroads throughout the South lay in ruins. The National Archives and the Library of Congress house a tremendous collection of photographs recording four years of repeated destruction, makeshift rebuilding, military misuse, and inadequate maintenance on both sides. Many Southern lines had lost as much as ninety percent of their former equipment. The New Orleans, Jackson, and Great Northern, which had been one of the best-equipped railroads of its time, had only four passenger cars left out of a former thirty-seven, two locomotives from a roster of forty-nine, thirty-six beat-up freight cars out of 550.

In the Northwest on the other hand, railroad construction continued during the war. On July 1, 1862, Congress passed the Pacific Railroad Act, authorizing the Union Pacific Railroad Company and granting it a 200-foot-wide right-of-way from Omaha west to San Francisco. An amendment to this Act also established four feet, 8½ inches as the standard gauge in the United States, a gauge which all major lines were forced to adopt around 1890. Abraham Lincoln opposed this, being in favor of the five-foot gauge. In 1863 the Atchinson, Topeka, and Santa Fe Railroad was granted a similar right-of-way along the 35th parallel latitude from Topeka west. Incidentally, a secondhand 4-4-0, originally built by Niles of Cincinnati for the Ohio and Mississippi Railroad, was the first locomotive to run on the new line, pulling a borrowed coach. The Santa Fe certainly has grown!

And so the rails moved westward from Chicago, from Independence, Galesburg, Topeka, Omaha, through territories "where every mile of the routes had to be laid within the protective range of the musket" (General Dodge, Union Pacific). One group of Cheyennes, who witnessed their first iron horse, tried to subdue the steaming beast with ponies. In a moment some twenty foolhardy but naive riders and their ponies lay dead. The memory of the blood-splashed cowcatcher created a lasting animosity toward the Union Pacific among the tribesmen, and many surveyors and section hands died by bow and arrow. In 1867 the Cheyennes captured a complete freight train and burned it in retaliation for the earlier pony versus iron horse episode.

But in spite of Indians, whiskey, and thugs, General Dodge's Irish tracklayers drove ten spikes per rail, laid four rails a minute, 400 rails to the mile, sometimes completing as much as seven miles of track per day!

Working east out of San Francisco, the Central Pacific overcame obstacles no other railroad had to face, and in six years laid its lines 690 miles east over the high Sierra Nevadas and the burning Nevada Desert. Thirty-one miles out of San Francisco the going got rugged. From there on the right-of-way over and through the Sierras had to be hacked out of solid granite with pick and shovel, aided by dangerous black powder charges

and little dump carts. Fourteen thousand Chinese coolies labored on the Bloomer Cut, chopped and blasted fifteen tunnels through conglomerate as hard as concrete.

The Central Pacific acquired its first locomotive, the "Governor Stanford," in 1863. It arrived on April 19, after a 15,000-mile trip around Cape Horn, on the clipper ship, "Herald of the Morning." The shipment also included rails, spikes, and the iron parts for a turntable. The wood-burning 4-4-0, built by Richard Norris and Sons of Philadelphia, was reassembled in Sacramento and made its maiden run pulling two flatcars full of dignitaries of state and county governments. From then on the "Governor Stanford" played a role in the construction boom of the 60's, and later served as a switcher in the Sacramento yards. The historic engine was presented to Stanford University in 1894 or 1899, and became covered with rubble in the great 1906 San Francisco earthquake. In 1916 it was partially restored and installed in a new museum. In 1952 the "Governor Stanford" was completely restored as nearly as possible to its original appearance. The uncertainty of the date and the poor condition of the available prints of the "Governor Stanford" in action are results of the 1906 earthquake.

Since no definite meeting place had been established, the grading crews of the Eastern and Western companies passed each other in the spring of 1869. The government finally stepped in and established the official meeting point at Promontory Point, Utah. Competition between the two construction gangs became fierce as the work neared its end. On October 19, 1868, the Union Pacific gaudy dancers laid 7½ miles of track east of Granger, Wyoming, which they believed the others could not equal, but on April 28, 1869, the Central laid ten miles and fifty-six feet of track between dawn and dark by almost superhuman effort. Inspired by a bet between Charles Crocker of the Central Pacific and U.P.'s Tom Durant, this record thinned down Durant's pocketbook by ten grand. Two days later the C.P. end of the line reached Promontory Point first. The Union Pacific was delayed by a difficult rock cut in the last five miles.

The rails from the east reached Promontory Point on Saturday, May 8. A gap of a few rail lengths between the Central Pacific and Union Pacific tracks was left for the final ceremonies on Monday. The C.P. officials and important men from the West had already arrived on May 6, bringing with them a highly polished cross-tie of California laurel, bearing a silver plaque, engraved with the legend, "The last tie laid on the completion of the Pacific Railroad, May, 1869." A beautiful golden spike was also brought along, and with it a fine silver hammer which was a gift of the Pacific Union Express Company. The golden spike, in size and shape much like a common one, was made at W. T. Garratts of San Francisco out of eighteen $20 gold pieces from the United States Mint there. The spike was engraved on one side with the inscription, "May God continue the unity of our country as this railroad unites the two great oceans of the world." Another side carried the words, "The Last Spike," followed by a list of the principal officials involved in the project. The third side was engraved with the names of the C.P.'s directors. The fourth side read, "The Central Pacific Railroad. Ground broken: January 8, 1863; Completed: May ——, 1869."

Coming from the East were Union Pacific's vice-president Thomas Durant, his directors, and other invited guests, including the Reverend Dr. John Todd of Pittsfield, Massachusetts. Their progress was hindered by discharged workmen, insisting on back wages before they would allow the train to proceed to Promontory Point.

On Monday morning, May 8, the two official trains approached Promontory from each direction: President Leland Stanford's, pulled by C.P. No. 60, a 4-4-0 named "Jupiter," and Thomas Durant's, pulled by 4-4-0 No. 119. The "Jupiter," a wood burner, had an enormous balloon stack which gave it a much more impressive appearance than the straight-stacked coal burner. A band from Ogden furnished appropriate music for the occasion. By noon the area around the historic spot was filled with spectators from nearby settlements, bishops of the Mormon Church, four companies of soldiers, the governors of Arizona and California, newspapermen and one photographer, plus the regular track-laying crews, totaling almost 1,500 men.

At noon Dr. Todd gave the invocation, which was followed by speeches. The golden spike was then handed to Stanford with a few appropriate remarks, and a silver spike, a gift from Nevada, placed in Durant's hands. A second golden spike, also a gift from California, and an alloy spike of gold, silver, and iron from Arizona, were also brought out. Durant and Stanford handled the silver sledge. Neither official succeeded in driving his spike into the tie. As if to prove that railroad management and construction work are totally different breeds, both men dented the fine silver maul on the track. Two chief engineers finished the job, and the telegraph ticked out for the benefit of waiting crowds in America's cities: "Done." It was 2:47 p.m. in the nation's capital.

The two locomotives, without their trains, then met pilot to pilot, and the enginemen each broke a bottle of champagne on the other's pilot. The 119 and the "Jupiter" then each in turn pulled their trains across this famous junction.

The pictures of the ceremony at Promontory Point are not too good, since all the original C.P. and Southern Pacific records were burned in the 1906 earthquake. Also the original laurel tie, on display at the general office, was lost at that time. Nevertheless, the records that remain prove once again the important part the 4-4-0's have played in our history.

Jan Gleysteen/'66

CHAPTER SEVEN

The Revival of a Classic

When I mentioned in an earlier chapter that the last 4-4-0 for domestic use was outshopped in 1928, I failed to reckon with the familiar saying, "You can't keep a good man down"—or for that matter, a locomotive. And so it happens that veritable 4-4-0's are again being manufactured, not thirty miles from my home, finding their way to railroads within and beyond our borders.

It all began like this: Ten years ago, in 1955, Ken Williams, a Pittsburgh area businessman with a deep-seated love for steam operation, noticed an ad for a 15-inch-gauge Cagney engine, offered for sale by a Charleston, South Carolina, amusement park. He could not resist the temptation and soon the sixty-year-old 4-4-0 arrived at its new home in Elizabeth Township. The little veteran, however, was in such poor shape that Ken Williams and his son Bert had to dismantle it and rebuild it again from the tracks up. While the engine now provided transportation for the Williams and their friends, it was remodeled and altered several more times, and later backdated to resemble a Civil War period locomotive.

In 1958 the Williams built their own experimental model and later that same year decided to go into the business of manufacturing miniature locomotives and cars. The first "Little Toot" 4-4-0 carrying the trademark Crown Metal Products was delivered in the spring of 1959. Since then the Little Toots have become rather popular and can be seen in many parts of the nation, from New Hampshire to Florida and from Ocean City to the Far West. They are bought by parks and estates as well as private collectors and hobbyists. No wonder, for this 15-inch-gauge replica of the 1865 has all the flavor and character of its larger prototype.

Sometime later Crown Metal began to offer two-foot-gauge American types, which are considerably more detailed and authentic. They were designed especially for parks and historic restorations with a wider track. The 24" is very popular with operators to whom a larger payload is important. This is only the second time that two-foot-gauge Americans have been built since Baldwin completed its one and only order for the three locomotives for the Mount Gretna Railroad way back in 1889. The Crown Metal two-footer ready to roll with a full load of coal and a tank of water weighs over 8,000 pounds. Running at a working boiler pressure of 175 pounds per square inch, and equipped with Bendix-Westinghouse Straight Air Brakes, this is no longer a toy related to the Cagney, yet it remains just as simple to operate. Its height is about 6½ feet from the railhead to the top of the generous balloon stack, and when you hear its whistle and its "stack-talk" beyond yonder hill, it is as if you are about to witness another Great Locomotive Chase.

One of the first 24-inches went to the Dry Gulch Railroad at the famous Hershey Park, Hershey, Pennsylvania. In its first season the little steamer hauled 250,000 passengers in the four coaches behind. Now in its fifth season the engine is in meticulous shape and fine mechanical condition, even though it still hauls thousands of children and their parents every year. Another Crown Metal two-footer in the 4-4-0 class makes a mile-long trip over the Hawthorn Mellody Farms Dairy at Libertyville, Illinois, through a lovely rural setting not too far from downtown Chicago.

As the name Crown Metal became known in the world of railroad enthusiasts, and associated with quality of workmanship, the inevitable was soon to happen: somebody wanted to place an order for a full-size American type to run on a three-foot-gauge line. While an engine this size could no longer be called Little Toot, Ken and Bert Williams seemed delighted with the challenge.

Pioneer locomotive designer William F. Kromer, now in his late 80's, who had been associated with the H. K. Porter Locomotive Works of Pittsburgh since 1904, was asked to produce the plans for the main specifications of the engine. This included driver diameter, size of the boiler, the dimensions of the cylinder, and other factors that determine the performance. In the meantime, the design consultants of the Crown Metal Products began to study thousands of Civil War and old Western Railroad photos, jotting down ideas and sketching interesting details that filled many sheets of paper. Some of these ideas were rejected as impractical, but out of the study emerged a synthesis of characteristics of an 1865 American.

Now the designers again went to work to add their findings to William Kromer's mechanical essentials, to scale a cab, to place the domes, to locate the bell, and to determine the shape of the tender. This design was completed and refined in July, 1962, while pattern-makers had already started to work on the stack and the more certain features. In the middle of September the three-foot-gauge locomotive, constructed in a hastily cleared implement shed, neared completion. It turned out to be even more beautiful than could be visualized from the meticulously-drawn blueprints; Ken Williams in his glory could be found near the engine at any time, doing just a little more pipefitting "just for recreation."

Early in October, 1962, the brand-new 4-4-0, as yet in a base coat of paint and unlettered, was trucked to Orbisonia, Pennsylvania, for test runs on the historic East Broad Top Railroad. Following or preceding the regularly scheduled E.B.T. trains up the line to Shirleysburg and back, the "brand-new-old" 4-4-0, coupled to one of the E.B.T. wooden cabooses, became a favorite target for the many photographers on hand. Frankly, many rail fans were puzzled and wondered aloud whether they were seeing ghosts.

The engine returned home to Elizabeth, Pennsylvania, for completion, corrections, and a resplendent paint and polish job. Several weeks later it left its birthplace for good. The twenty-five-ton 4-4-0 was firmly secured on a Pennsylvania Railroad flatcar and headed south from Pittsburgh. Its passage through the South to its new home in Silver Springs, Florida, was duly noted by newspapers and TV; a cargo like that couldn't help but attract a lot of attention. The owners of Crown Metal's first full-scale eight-wheeler were so pleased with its performance and looks that they ordered a second one. And now, locomotives No. 4 and 7, almost identical but in different livery, each haul as many as 2,000 passengers per hour in open-sided-excursion coaches.

Shortly thereafter the 4-4-0 "Tempe Arizona" was built for the Legend City Railroad near Phoenix, Arizona. Today Crown Metal Products is the leader in the steam locomotive business, producing mostly 4-4-0's but occasionally a larger-type engine. A new erecting shop near the Williams farm home, which has long since replaced the old shed as a center of activity, has room for quite a few locomotives on its floor. Besides locomotives, coaches and cabooses, air brakes, bridge and trackwork, the Crown Metal Products Co. also supplies replacement parts for steam-operated railways around the world. John Barriger, former president of the Pittsburgh & Lake Erie Railroad, once remarked, "Isn't it remarkable that the largest steam locomotive works in the States today wasn't even in business when we completed the dieselization of the P. & L. E."

Even though the business has grown, it is still operated as a family business. Ken's wife, Elsie, and Bert's wife, Mary Lynn, are active participants in the company. To Elsie goes the credit for much of the decor and the color schemes used on the trains.

For Ken Williams, a friendly person with laughter in his eyes, the imaginative enterprise still seems to be as much his hobby as his business. This could be the influence of both heredity and environment. He was born above the quarters of a remote depot on the Canadian National, at Ninette, Manitoba, where his father was agent. He grew up "well within the sound of the telegraph key" and at the age of fifteen became a full-time railroader. Although his several careers since he left the railroad in 1926 and came to the United States have included printing, farming, and manufacturing, Ken has always maintained a special love for steam railroads. Evidence of this can be found throughout the Williams farm and home in Elizabeth Township, and in his office at Wyano, which is appropriately housed in a large double-lounge Pullman observation car parked on a spur. Ken Williams is a well-read person who loves to share his fascination with trains and Americana with you in the hospitable surroundings of his home or office. But unlike most others, he and his family have turned this interest into a growing business of producing these replicas out of a romantic past, the Crown Metal 4-4-0's.

CHAPTER EIGHT

Models, Music, and Masterpieces

The eight-wheelers were so predominant on the American scene, and played such a vital part in history, that it is only natural that their likeness shows up in a multitude of forms and places, from stamps to greeting cards, from wooden pull toys to highly detailed scale models, in the fine arts and as decoration on household articles. Once alerted, you begin to notice 4-4-0's everywhere in varying degrees of accuracy.

The most obvious replicas are the toy locomotives which later developed into super-detailed exhibition pieces. In the New England museums and antique shops I have occasionally seen wooden pull toys with glued-on lithographed paper sides, which included 4-4-0's and their coaches. In the 1880's cast-iron trackless locomotives were first made in Connecticut. The manufacturers of these were Carpenter, Ives, Wilkins, Stevens, all of Connecticut, and the Grey Iron Casting Co. of Mount Joy, Pennsylvania. Some of these cast iron engines were quite large and in some cases excellent in scale. They were widely available until World War I. From 1890 on they were made with or without clockwork motors. After the record of the 999, New York Central locomotives furnished the prototype. The first live steam models built by Beggs in 1870 were large and elaborate 4-4-0's that ran on wooden tracks.

In 1900 the Weeden Company produced a live steam 4-4-0 in 0 gauge, named "Dart." The German Märklin Co. also exported some live steam 4-4-0's which, in spite of pilots and bells, and P.R.R. initials, continued to look very European.

From 1900 on, Ives, Dorfan, Bing, Boucher, Howard, Märklin, and Voltamp produced electric trains with 4-4-0 engines, side by side with their clockwork and live steam sets. One of the nicest ones was a 1927 Ives electric locomotive for $2\frac{1}{8}$ inch track, modeled after the Baltimore and Ohio's "President Washington." Only Lionel, a famous name in later years, shied away from the American type, although between 1906 and 1923 the very handsome No. 6 and No. 7 were mar-

keted. Instead, Lionel concentrated its efforts on the more obscure Columbia type, of which only 140 prototypes were ever built, mostly for the Burlington.

The past twenty-five years have brought us more detailed models and true-scale masterpieces. In the beginning the difference between toys (or tinplate) and scale was not as great as it is now, and what was regarded as a scale model in 1930 probably does not meet present-day standards.

In 1941 Rollin J. Lobaugh, a great name in scale railroading, brought out an excellent 0 gauge model of a New Haven Railroad 4-4-0, also available in kit form. In 1959 the Lionel Corporation produced a truly superb replica of the "General" and its train, complete with an illuminated box-type headlight and a smoking balloon stack. After this great contribution to 0 gauge railroading, Lionel continued its downward trend with more exploding missile cars and a flood of militaristic nonsense. From an unexpected source, Louis Marx, more noted for its tinplate trains, came a very nice model of the "William Crooks," the first locomotive in Minnesota. The short-lived Thomas Industries also produced a classic 4-4-0 with clean lines. It sported a tricky box light of frosted lucite that looked for all the world like a glowing oil lamp. Thanks to the Civil War Centennial all 4-4-0 old-timers were popular items.

In HO models the 4-4-0 is even more readily available. The excellent reproductions of the Virginia and Truckee engines "Genoa" and "Reno" brought out by AHM of Philadelphia are the first that come to mind. They are rich in detail and should be the center of attraction on anybody's model pike. Earlier Mantua marketed the "Belle of the Eighties," and still sells the "General" under the Tyco trademark.

The famous "General" of the Great Locomotive Chase is probably the most reproduced locomotive. The Rosebud Kitmaster Company of England produced it in an inexpensive but well-detailed kit. A European firm,

Kitmaster also produced kits of the famous British 4-4-0's: the "City of Truro," which held the speed record for Europe in 1904, and the locomotive "Harrow" of the "Schools" class. Triang Railways, another British manufacturer, offers a meticulous class 3P inside-connected 4-4-0 complete with double-line pinstriping.

In 0 gauge the world-famous firm of Bassett-Lowke of Northampton, England, offers the inside-connected 4-4-0 "Prince Charles," a L.M.R. compound, based on the "Derby" class 4-4-0's of 1823, and the 4-4-0 "Enterprise" in live steam. The "Enterprise" is a free-lance design based on standard British features. It is also available in kit form. At the time of this writing, none of the continental manufacturers lists 4-4-0's in their catalogs.

In the development of outdoor railways no one played a more important role than the four Cagney brothers of Jersey City, New Jersey. In 1894 the foursome, Timothy G., David H., Charles L., and Thomas G. Cagney, brought out a smaller version of New York Central's 999. As they had foreseen, young and old were indeed delighted with the thought of riding behind a miniature of the famous speed king. They were by far the best-looking miniatures on the market. Over 3,000 were built in 15-inch or 22-inch gauge.

The heyday of the Cagneys was right after World War I, when the little but powerful 4-4-0's steamed through parks all over the United States, in Siam, in Russia, in South Africa, and the Latin-American countries. A few served a more utilitarian purpose on steamship piers or on contractors' railways. Partly because of labor union problems in the park business, the Cagney company declined to the point of extinction. But the engines are still being bought and sold, reboilered and modified. Yet somehow they always remain recognizable as the durable little Cagneys.

If you are ever in the neighborhood of Lomita, California, I suggest you visit Mrs. Irene Lewis, who operates a most unusual business in her backyard. In a neat Quonset hut factory she and a crew of three build live steam 4-4-0's of a handsome proportion. Mrs. Lewis, a widow, is the only woman graduate from the International Correspondence School course in loco-motive engineering, and to judge by the performance of the $4\frac{3}{4}$ gauge steamers traversing her yard, she graduated cum laude. Her 4-4-0, one of many models available, is a bolt-together-kit, which requires only simple hand tools to complete.

Up in Wisconsin Dells, Wisconsin, the Sandleys have produced an excellent 15-inch-gauge 4-4-0, the "L. W. Nieman," No. 82 on the Milwaukee Zoo Railroad. While this engine, a gift from the "Milwaukee Journal," was built with an obvious love for detail and finish, there is no record of further 4-4-0-type engines built by the Sandley Light Railway Equipment Works.

Let us turn from the 4-4-0 in three-dimensional state and examine their appearance in the arts. In music and song, of course, it is hard to ascertain the class of engine glorified, unless you happen to know that the "Wabash Cannonball" was pulled by Americans. In the case of the old Southern ballad, "The 29," we do know that Will S. Hays wrote the poem, later set to music, after admiring Thatcher Perkins' beautifully designed "Southern Belle," No. 29 on the Louisville and Nashville, and mentions this in the refrain.

The hero of the widely translated Polish children's classic, "Lokomotywa," by Julian Tuwim, is obviously a very black and oily, but able 4-4-0, delightfully pictured by Jan Szancer. In England the Reverend W. Awdry, in his dozen or more children's books in the Railway Series, frequently features a 4-4-0 in Caledonian blue named "Edward." He devoted booklet No. 9 exclusively to Edward's adventures.

In the visual arts the 4-4-0 is far easier to identify. The 4-4-0 is a predominant feature in the lithographs of Currier and Ives, the famous printmakers of the last century. Thanks to Currier and Ives, and their usual accuracy, we have some idea of what the earliest 4-4-0's looked like in the days before photography. One very old print, by N. Currier, undated but before his affiliation with Ives, shows us just such an engine, still without a headlight, but with a cab and plenty of gray woodsmoke leaving the "Dolly Varden" stack. The time may be around 1850.

Later Currier and Ives turned out a sizable repertoire of prints of Americans under all circumstances: The American Express Train (in many versions), The Lightning Express, The Danger Signal, Night Scene at an American Junction, Lookout Mountain, and the Chattanooga Railroad—all carefully drawn, numbered, and lettered down to very last coach. For stock lithographs of locomotives, Atlantic and Great Western locomotive No. 16 often posed for the artist-partners.

In 1867 Edward Lamson Henry, a noted New England painter, immortalized the "9:45 Accommodation, Stratford, Connecticut," showing a typical depot scene right after the arrival of an ornate and colorful 4-4-0 and a string of yellow coaches. The hustle and bustle of arrival and departure under an uncertain spring sky are very well portrayed. The painting is now in the Metropolitan Museum of Art in New York.

About the same time N. H. Trotter painted a timid-looking green 4-4-0 with a diamond stack stopped on the Western prairies to wait out the passing of an immense sea of buffaloes, hoping that the stampeding herd would not derail any of the light coaches behind it. This painting hangs in the Smithsonian Institute.

We find three artists of name among the railroad painters of today. The veteran among them is artist-railroader Otto Kuhler, born in Cologne, Germany. In 1923, after he had already constructed and operated a railroad in Belgium and graduated from the Royal Academy of Art in Düsseldorf, he arrived in Pittsburgh, Pennsylvania. By the light of a kerosene lamp he designed a streamline train for the American Car & Foundry Company, and a streamline locomotive for the American Locomotive Company. By 1931 he was design consultant for the Alco, for whom he designed some of the finest luxury trains, including B. & O.'s "Capitol Limited." All the while he continued to etch and paint. Otto Kuhler now lives on a ranch in Colorado, where he devotes all his time to painting and printmaking. Kuhler is represented in this book with a recent painting entitled "Train to Trinidad," showing a Colorado and Wyoming 4-4-0 on its way north to Walsenburg, Pueblo, and Denver around 1910. Howard Fogg of Boulder, Colorado, is famous for his series of sixty-five watercolors painted between 1956 and 1964 for the Pittsburgh and Lake Erie Railroad. One of these paintings, showing the 999 in action, is reproduced in this book.

Calendar artist Paul Detlefsen, now living in Hawaii, continuing to paint nostalgic Americana, seems to be very much in favor of letting 4-4-0's disturb the quiet of his pastoral scenery. Detlefsen is a model railroader of high repute as well.

In commercial art and illustration the 4-4-0 is frequently used to create a period piece, and the greeting card companies have multiplied the trusty eight-wheeler a million times. If at Christmas you cannot find at least ten 4-4-0 inspired cards, printed in full color, embossed and die-cut, all or not trimmed with evergreen, you are not really looking.

Stamp collections have been called "Miniature Art Galleries," and in these galleries the 4-4-0 is once more well represented. The United States featured the world record holder 999 on a two-cent commemorative stamp in 1901, on the occasion of the Pan-American Exposition. In 1944 the seventy-fifth anniversary of the completion of the transcontinental railroad at Promontory Point, Utah, was remembered on a purple three-cent stamp. It showed the ceremony in front of Central Pacific's engine, "Jupiter." In 1948 a century of U.S.-Canadian friendship was the occasion for a light blue stamp showing the Niagara Railway Suspension Bridge. Too small to be identified from the stamp, we know the locomotive on the bridge to be a broad-gauge, balloon-stacked 4-4-0 of the Great Western Railway. The Canal Zone issued a commemorative stamp in 1955 for the 100th anniversary of the Panama Railroad showing two early 4-4-0's and their trains. Of the second engine only the stack is visible.

Honduras, Cuba, Brazil, and Chile each have stamps with 4-4-0's. The two Chile stamps in the values of $1.00 and $10.00 are as beautiful as stamps come, and show the detail of a U.S.-built 4-4-0 with the fidelity of a builder's photo. Cuba's unusual stamp of 1950 shows a 4-4-0 involved in a wreck with more recent diesel equipment. Belgium's four-franc stamp, one of a series of eighteen locomotive stamps, shows a T18 class 4-4-0 of 1910, and Baldwin's first locomotives for Finland are featured on a very nice 1962 stamp of that country.

The American type is shown even more frequently on paper money. One of the reasons is that prior to 1862 most anybody could issue paper currency: banks and insurance companies as well as the railroads. Such a private dollar bill was seldom worth a dollar in those days, but rather was equal to a certain amount of merchandise or transportation. A dollar bill might read: "South Carolina Railroad Company. Good for fare of one passenger over twenty-five miles. Charleston, July 7, 1873." Most of these bills have attractive engravings of locomotives on them, almost without exception American types, then in their height of glory. Between 1854 and 1857 approximately 300 million dollars of railroad money were issued, which was equal to four times the national debt of those days.

Returning once more to the fine arts, we find a few sculptures and bas-reliefs of eight-wheelers. By far the most significant is a forty-foot wood carving by the Arizona artist Dee Flagg, portraying "Jesse James' Last Great Train Robbery, 1881." It was begun after months of concentrated research and preparation. The amount of detail Dee Flagg coaxed out of the wood is terrific, including bits of slugs in the splintered baggage door, and yet he has been able to keep the action alive and spontaneous. The locomotive is Rock Island's famous Silver Engine, "America."

The other sculptures are mostly monuments, including the Andrews' Raid Monument in the National Cemetery, Chattanooga, Tennessee. This was a gift from the state of Ohio in honor of the raiders. A bas-relief in marble, showing a Norris 4-4-0 locomotive of 1856, is one of the hundreds of memorial stones inside the Washington Monument, probably largely unnoticed by the thousands of weary climbers trying to make it to the top. The first 4-4-0 equipped with air brakes is prominently featured on the center panel of a memorial in Schenley Park, Pittsburgh, Pennsylvania, depicting the contributions of George Westinghouse. Yes, in a thousand forms, the 4-4-0 will live forever!

CHAPTER NINE

The American Abroad

Of the 25,600 American types built in the United States, only about 600, or less than three percent, were exported. Among them were some of the very early models: the Baldwins for the Finnish Railways in 1862, the locomotives for the Veronej-Rostoff line in Russia, some interesting Baldwin products with inclined cylinders for Norway and numerous orders from north and south of our borders. Eastwick and Harrison moved its entire operation to Russia to start on an order for 100 locomotives after their "Gowan & Marx" proved the possibilities of the 4-4-0 wheel arrangement. For almost a century small orders for American types were placed by such lines as the Hankaku Railway and the Hokkaido Colliery and Railway, both of Japan, the New South Wales Government Railways of Australia, the Yeh Han line of China, the Ferrocarriles Internacionales de Centro America, and others. The very last 4-4-0's, built in 1946, were eleven Baldwin engines for the Ferrocarrilles Unidos de Yucatan (Mexico), which still make their daily rounds between Merida and Progreso, or from Merida to the famous Chichen Itza ruins. The locomotives haul bananas, hemp, and coffee, as well as passengers. In total seventeen 4-4-0's were built for this sunny part of Mexico over the past eighty years. U. de Y. 4-4-0 No. 351, built in 1887, still occasionally delivers the goods at sixty-five miles per hour—not bad for an octogenarian.

If only 600 American types went beyond our borders, we may not conclude that the 4-4-0's were not as widely used as here. In fact, they were every bit as popular. Locomotives of this wheel arrangement were built in England, Holland, Germany, and other European countries for domestic use and for export. A few British-built 4-4-0's even came to America. An example was the Great Western locomotive "Spitfire," which despite balloon stack, wooden cab, and pilot still looked very British.

The roster of the Netherlands Railways alone showed 428 engines of the 4-4-0 type, many of which served till the end of steam traction in the lowlands. Quite a variety of 4-4-0's still serve England's nationalized railways, around the docks of Spanish harbors, in the outback of Australia, and through New Zealand's primeval forests. In this chapter we will tactfully refrain from calling them "Americans," but continue to describe their everpresence and their achievements.

Great Britain, like the United States, first had a multitude of gauges, from three- to seven-feet wide. In the United States this battle of the gauges was settled by law as part of the Railroad Act of 1862, establishing the gauge of four feet 8½ inches as standard. A Royal Commission had recommended this track width two decades earlier, in 1845, on the basis of tests. The odd measurement dates back to Bible times, and had come to England either through the Romans or the Crusaders as the customary distance between wagon wheels.

But for about twenty more years two rival gauges existed side by side in England, while in the United States the railroads tried to ignore the problem by using so-called "compromise cars," that could run (but not very well) on two gauges. This system was responsible for more than its share of the many wrecks that plagued the early railroads. When finally forty-nine people died in a wreck near Angola, New York, because of a Lake Shore and Michigan Southern compromise car, public outrage forced the nonconforming lines to change over.

It was for the seven-foot gauge Great Western Railway that Daniel Gooch, already known as a master craftsman in British circles, designed a series of 4-4-0's, which were built by the father of the locomotive, Robert Stephenson, in 1855. Gooch's 4-4-0's were intended for the faster trains between Swindon and South Wales, where severe gradients existed. The huge engines had seven-foot driving wheels and inside connected cylinders. This was the beginning of a predominance of 4-4-0's on Britain's high iron, and an era of service that hasn't ended yet. Still in the same year,

35

HUNTINGTON CITY TOWNSHIP
PUBLIC LIBRARY
255 WEST PARK DRIVE
HUNTINGTON, IN 46750

Stephenson constructed five 4-4-0 tank engines for the North London Railway, the world's first 4-4-0t's. Right from the beginning we see two developments which became more popular in Europe than over here: inside-connected cylinders for smoother running and tank engines (locomotives without tenders, equipped to haul fuel and water in bunkers and tanks surrounding the cab). Tank engines, which needed no turning, were excellent for local and branch-line runs.

In 1860 Stephenson delivered six 4-4-0's to the Stockton and Darlington Railway with outside cylinders and American-type cabs. In 1861 the Stephenson 4-4-0 was chosen standard engine for the Great North of Scotland Railway. Four years later this railway installed Adams spring-controlled leading trucks on all its 4-4-0's to minimize any side motion.

In 1864 Messieurs Beyer, Peacock and Company, one of the great names in locomotive construction, delivered the first of 148 4-4-0's for the London Metropolitan Railway. An unusual feature of these engines was a condensing apparatus which bypassed the exhaust steam back into the tank.

Between 1863 and 1869 William Adams built some 4-4-0t's fitted with his improved spring-controlled sliding bogie for the North London Railway. So successful were these engines that the 4-4-0's remained standard motive power on that line until the day of electrification.

From 1871 onwards there was a gradual development of the 4-4-0 engine in England, chiefly in Scotland. The first examples of what is now Standard British type were built in 1871 by the North British Railway from designs developed by Thomas Wheatley. Superintendent D. Drummond adopted this class as standard on the N.B.R. in 1876, and the London, Chatham, and Dover followed suit in 1877. By 1880 the 4-4-0 was much favored on all lines. The South Eastern Railway bought 117 standard eight-wheelers in one year. Around this time the inside cylinders were abandoned for most classes of locomotives, except the 4-4-0.

In 1889 Dugald Drummond, now serving the famous Caledonian Railway, experimentally upped the steam pressure to 200 pounds per square inch. Ten years later the London and North Eastern Railway introduced the "1620" class of 4-4-0's which had a working boiler pressure of 200 pounds and 91-inch drivers. These were the largest wheels ever to appear on a 4-4-0. The "1620" class was built for competitive runs to Scotland.

In 1895 one of the greatest classes of 4-4-0's, the "Dunalastair" class was conceived and born in the Caledonian Railway Shops in Glasgow. Its creator was designer John Farquharson McIntosh, Locomotive, Car-

riage, and Wagon Superintendent from 1895 to 1914. His "Dunalastair" class, named after a Scottish estate, was way out front in efficiency, robustness, and power output in relation to size. For this accomplishment King George V named McIntosh a member of the Royal Victorian Order in 1913, in recognition of his "sterling services in the field of locomotive design and to his country."

The "Dunalastair" type underwent about five major changes and improvements between 1895 and 1914, and so we find classifications like the "Dunalastair IV, superheater class." Altogether, eighty-seven engines of this type were placed in service on the Caledonian.

The "Dunalastairs" were not only efficient, but beautiful as well. Under Caledonian ownership they were spotlessly clean and polished to perfection. Painted Prussian blue, and sky blue after 1906, with gloss black smokebox and frames, lined with bands of black bordered with white pinstriping, sporting a blue Westinghouse Air Brake edged in white, and adorned with the Caledonian coat of arms on the leading splasher, they were a pleasant sight to behold. The initials "C.R." on the tender were in gold leaf shaded in reds and blacks and highlighted in white. According to standard British practice, the buffer beams were vermilion red with white initials and number.

On July 1, 1923, the Caledonian Railway became part of the L.M.S. and the "Dunalastairs" were painted in an ill-maintained Midland red, followed in 1948 by the even drabber and badly kept black of the nationalized British Railways. One of the "Dunalastairs" still running in Scotland has been selected for a full working restoration in the original Caledonian livery, after which she will join her sister 4-4-0's and other engines in Britain's museum collection.

Engines Nos. 48 and 121 of the superheated "Dunalastair IV" class, double heading a troop train on May 22, 1915, had the unenviable distinction of being involved in one of the world's worst train disasters. In a collision near Quintinshill, 227 persons, nearly all soldiers of the Royal Scots battalions, were killed and another 245 badly injured. One reason the toll was so high was that the wrecked train caught fire from the gas lighting system in the coaches.

In 1903 W. Dean designed the "City" class engines with inside cylinders for the Great Western Railway. They were handsome engines with Belpaire fireboxes and wagon-type boilers. Of this class the "City of Truro" reached a verified speed of 102.3 miles per hour on May 9, 1904, with a special train between Plymouth and London's Paddington Station.

The "City of Truro" was the two thousandth locomotive built at the Great Western Railway Works at

Swindon. The locomotive was withdrawn from service in 1931 and preserved in the York Railway Museum until early 1957. It was then renovated in the old Great Western Railway livery used at the early part of the century, and placed back into service. Its use was restricted to working special excursion trains run in connection with certain railway activities. Now, withdrawn from service again, it is appropriately preserved in the new railway museum at Swindon.

Another successful 4-4-0 was built in 1913 to replace a larger class of engines in use on the Great Central Railway. This group of eight-wheelers, known as the "Directors" class, eventually numbered 44 engines. They were named after the directors of the company and, like the "Dunalastairs," lasted well into the days of the British Railways. An unusual feature was the absence of a drawbar between the engine and its tender. It was instead coupled with a shackle and two chains. The engine itself ran beautifully, but the tender danced all over the track as if trying to part with the engine. Much of the fireman's precious energy was spent in shoveling the shifting coal back into its proper place on the tender.

When the "Directors" class was phased out in 1962, engine No. 506, the "Butler Henderson," was also restored to the original Great Central livery of green with maroon and black trim, and is now stored in London.

In 1924 the L.M.S. ordered 140 compound 4-4-0's and fifty simple 4-4-0's with superheaters to be used as standard locomotives on their lines, and in 1930 the Southern Railway placed an order for the first of the famous "Schools" class 4-4-0's. These engines were the most powerful 4-4-0's in the world. Seeing a "Schools" class engine for the first time, you would have to convince yourself that you were not looking at a much larger or heavier type of engine. With names chosen from the famous schools, such as "Eton," "Dulwich," "Harrow," "Sevenoaks," "Kings Canterbury," "Radley," etc., these engines were assigned to the express trains from London to Dover, Hastings, and Portsmouth, replacing the heavier "King Arthur" class.

These engines had very pleasing lines and no major alterations to the design were ever necessary, except for the addition of smoke deflectors alongside the smokebox to prevent a downdraft of smoke and steam that could obscure the crews' visibility. During the war, one of the "Schools" class locomotives was provided with an armored cab, but it was found unnecessary to fit out further engines, once the R.A.F. planes turned the tide of war.

The "Schools" class locomotives were the last 4-4-0's built in England, but a few of them and other 4-4-0's can still be seen on the British Railways, although they are now black and unbespeakably grimy. A total of 1615 4-4-0's were among the property nationalized in 1948. Two of the remaining 4-4-0's are Nos. 62614 and 62619 of the "Claud" class assigned to the Royal Train at Kings Lynn. (The 4-4-0's of the "Claud" class have been assigned to the Royal Train since 1900.) The two engines are identical to sister locomotives on duty, except for a telephone conduit through the tender for communication with the train, and a permanently assigned shift of four engineers and four firemen.

So much for Great Britain, which is after all the birthplace of the locomotive. Over on the mainland other 4-4-0's happily plied, and in some cases still run, their assigned routes. The firms of Richard Hartman, Krauss-Maffei, Dubs & Co., Werkspoor, A. Börsig, Beyer and Peacock, Ltd., Nydquist & Holm, Winterthur, Henschel, Jung, etc., are the Baldwins and the Masons of Europe. In many cases the railroads also built their own 4-4-0's and, especially in Holland and Italy, were given to much experimentation. Different value gears were tried out on the 4-4-0, and they were given different diets of coal, lignite, or even peat. Italy produced some awfully ugly specimens, loaded with experimental additions and piping. And where else but in Belgium would you find a 4-4-0 with a square smokestack?

In Switzerland open-cab 4-4-0's conquered the Simplon and the Jura in daily ascents until the days of electrification. In France "Outrance" class 4-4-0's hauled the famed Calais Boat Trains. The late Kaiser Wilhelm II left nothing to chance: his "Kaiserlicher Hofzug" was always pulled by two 4-4-0's. In 1913 W. Hupkes, later president of the Netherlands Railways, designed the largest 4-4-0's in Europe at that time, later surpassed by the "Schools" class. They were the 500 series of the Hollandsche IJzeren Spoorweg Maatschappij, which had a maximum allowable weight of 17.5 tons per axle. A few of these 500's were outfitted in 1934 with forerunners of the later Scullin disc driving wheels.

And so, 130 years after the pioneer 4-4-0 clanked down the middle of a Philadelphia cobblestone street, a few of its descendants still serve in the far-out corners of the world. Perhaps the most interesting use of a 4-4-0 today is found on the Fiji Islands. Here a diminutive outside-frame Beyer and Peacock provides free passenger service over the length of the island, going southbound in the morning and returning home at night. There are no stations on the sixty-mile round trip, but whenever necessary the train slows down, and while it is still in motion the passengers hop aboard the opensided cars. The two terminals are Ba and Lautoka. The main purpose of the line is to provide transportation for the island's sugar-cane traffic.

CHAPTER TEN

Lone Survivors

Railroads, like human beings, are better endowed with hindsight than foresight. This is most obvious in the field of documentation and preservation. Naturally it would be impossible to maintain a large collection of steam engines, coaches, freight cars, buildings, and equipment, but an effort should have been made to preserve for future generations a choice roster of typical as well as famous engines. This has not been done. As a result the railroads and museums now often have to resort to "faking"—rebuilding and/or repainting similar engines to look like the holder of the speed record, or the first engine in a certain state. Examples are: Casey Jones' engine No. 382, at Jackson, Tennessee, which is really a sister engine of a different number; the Pennsylvania E2 Atlantic No. 7002, stored at Northumberland, Pennsylvania, which is really a redone E7 Atlantic; and the "Jupiter" of Promontory Point fame, which is really Virginia and Truckee Railroad No. 12, quite unlike the real "Jupiter." In other cases the railroads have built working replicas of their historic locomotives. The "John Stevens" (P.R.R.), the "Stourbridge Lion" (D.&H.), the "Tom Thumb" (B.&O.), the "Best Friend of Charleston" (Southern), and the DeWitt Clinton (N.Y.C.) are among the replicas around the country. The cost of building replicas is, of course, almost prohibitive, and it remains a question whether more or larger replicas will ever be built.

In some cases valuable engines were preserved for a time, only to be scrapped later. The historic "Sabine," a Southern Pacific 4-4-0, was restored in 1923 and placed in a park at Lafayette, Louisiana. Then, twenty years later, in the passion of the moment, the Sabine was donated to the schoolboys' scrap metal drive, a move now bitterly regretted by the Southern Pacific and local citizens. The beginning of a promising railroad museum at Lexington, Kentucky, suffered the same fate. A pitifully small amount of usable iron was gained at the expense of a historical artifact of no mean importance. It took considerable effort to save even such famous engines as the "General" from the overzealous scrap enthusiasts.

Today, steam locomotives have become rather scarce and it is easy to keep track of the remaining ones. Among the survivors are some forty American types, a few of them replicas. In addition a number of 4-4-0's survive beyond our borders. For your convenience their location and history are listed below. You may wish to include them in your vacation plans.

UNITED STATES

ALABAMA: **Chapman:** (between Montgomery and Brewton) W. T. Smith Lumber Co., Railroad No. 14, built 1913.

ARIZONA: **Phoenix:** Legend City No. 1, "Tempe Arizona," built by Crown Metal Products in 1963.

CALIFORNIA: **Los Angeles:** Disneyland No. 1, "C. K. Holliday," and No. 2, "E. P. Ripley," both built in 1955.

Los Angeles: Griffith Park. Stockton Termnial and Eastern No. 1. Built in 1864, this locomotive was in continuous service for 89 years until its retirement and preservation in 1953.

Los Angeles: Union Pacific Roundhouse. Virginia and Truckee Railroad No.18 "Dayton", ex-Central Pacific, 1872 and Virginia and Truckee Railroad No. 22, "Inyo", a Baldwin product of 1875. Both owned by Paramount pictures.

Los Angeles: Warner Brothers movie lot: Hobart Southern No. 5, Baldwin 1881, 3-foot gauge. MGM movie lot: Virginia and Truckee Railroad No. 11, "Reno," Baldwin 1872.

Oakland: North Pacific Coast Railroad No. 12 "Sonoma," and Virginia and Truckee Railroad No. 12 "Genoa." Both engines are stored at the Western Pacific roundhouse and may be seen by appointment.

San Francisco: Bethlehem Steel Co. North Western Pacific Railroad No. 112, built 1908.

San Francisco: Maritime Museum. Central Pacific No. 1: "Governor Stanford" built 1863.

CONNECTICUT: **Danbury:** Boston and Providence Railroad "Daniel Nason," built 1856.

DELAWARE: **Wilmington:** Wilmington and Western Railroad. Former Mississippi Central locomotive No. 101.

DISTRICT OF COLUMBIA: **Washington:** John F. Kennedy Playground. International Railways of Central America No. 84, built 1876, in service till 1963.

FLORIDA: **Fort Lauderdale:** Pioneer City. No. 3 "Jenny Lynn," built by Crown Metal in 1964.

Silver Springs: Six Gun Territory No. 4 "General Sam Houston" and No. 7 "General Robert E. Lee," built by Crown Metal in 1962 and 1963.

GEORGIA: **Atlanta:** Cyclorama: Western and Atlantic "Texas."

Atlanta: Six Flags over Georgia. 3-foot gauge reproductions of the "General" and the "Texas," built by Harpur of Wilmington, California.

Atlanta: Stone Mountain Scenic Railway. Ex-Louisiana and Eastern No. 1, the "General II," and Ex-Talbottom Railroad No. 349, now the "Texas II," both built in the early 1920's.

ILLINOIS: **Chicago:** Museum of Science and Industry. New York Central's speed queen, the 999 on display. Built 1893.

MARYLAND: **Baltimore:** B. & O. Museum. The "William Mason," B. & O. No. 25, built in 1856.

MICHIGAN: **Dearborn:** Henry Ford Museum, Greenfield Village. Atlantic and Gulf Railroad "Sam Hill," built 1860. Lake Shore and Michigan Central No. 1, built 1868. Detroit, Toledo and Ironton No. 7, built 1897. Toledo-Detroit Railroad No. 16, built 1915.

MINNESOTA: **St. Paul:** Union Depot. Great Northern No. 1, "William Crooks," built 1861.

MISSOURI: **St. Louis:** National Museum of Transport. Chicago and North Western No. 274, built 1873. Boston and Albany Railroad No. 39 "Marmora," built 1876. Delaware, Lackawanna & Western No. 952, a camelback 4-4-0, built 1905. Missouri, Kansas, Texas Railroad No. 311, built in 1890.

St. Louis (Eureka): Six Flags over Mid-America. No. 5 and No. 6, built in 1969 by Crown Metal Products.

NEBRASKA: **Omaha:** Henry Doorley Zoo. 30 inch gauge replica of Union Pacific's Golden Spike engine, the 119. Built by Crown Metal Products, Wyano, Pennsylvania in 1968.

NEW JERSEY: **Allaire:** Pine Creek Railroad. "Lady Edith" a 4-4-0t built by Stephenson in 1887. Ex-Cavan and Leitrim Railway, Ireland.

NORTH CAROLINA: **Cherokee:** Frontierland No. 2 "Sequoyah," built in 1963 by Crown Metal.

OREGON: **Portland:** Portland Zoo. No. 1 "Oregon," built in 1959.

PENNSYLVANIA: **Philadelphia:** Franklin Institute. People's Railway No. 3, built in 1842, oldest 4-4-0 in existence.

Strasburg: Strasburg Rail Road. Ex-Louisiana and Eastern No. 98, built in 1909. Also a P.R.R. D16b on loan, No. 1223, built in 1905.

TENNESSEE: **Chattanooga:** Western and Atlantic No. 3, the "General," built 1855.

TEXAS: **El Paso:** Texas Western College. El Paso and South Western (now S.P.) No. 1. Built 1859.

VERMONT: **Bellows Falls:** Steamtown Foundation. Ex-Erath Sugar Co., built ca. 1880. Also a

Schools Class 4-4-0 "Repton," built 1930 Ex-British Railways.

WASHINGTON:
White River Junction: Municipal Building. Boston and Maine No. 494, built 1892.
Pasco: Volunteer Park. Northern Pacific No. 684, built 1883.

CANADA

BRITISH COLUMBIA: **Vancouver:** No. 374, first engine in the Canadian West, 1887.

MANITOBA: **Winnipeg:** No. 1 "Countess of Dufferin" built in 1872. First engine in Winnipeg. Now displayed in front of C.P.R. station.
Winnipeg: City of Winnipeg Hydro No. 3 built in 1882, was in service till 1964.

QUEBEC: **Montreal:** Canadian Pacific engines No. 136 and No. 144 built in 1883, C.P. engine No. 29, built in 1887. All served till 1962.

MEXICO

YUCATAN: **Merida** and **Progreso:** Ferrocarrilles Unidos de Yucatan engines Nos. 68, 251, 350, 351, still in regular service, possibly thirteen other 4-4-0's in storage.

BRAZIL

Interior of Brazil: "Col. Church," Baldwin 1880, 42-inch gauge.

EUROPE

DENMARK: **Copenhagen:** Railway Museum. One class A, two class K, one class C 4-4-0's are preserved. Numbers not available.

IRELAND: **Belfast:** Transport Museum. NCC No. 74 "Dunluce Castle."

GREAT BRITAIN: **Clapham:** Great Central No. 506 "Butler Henderson." London Midland & Southern No. 1000. Southeastern and Chatham Railroad No. 737. London and Southwestern No. 563.
Swindon: Great Western No. 3440 "City of Truro," holder of British and European speed record.
York: Railway Museum. North Eastern No. 1621.
British Railways: in storage at various places, restored or scheduled for restoration: London and Southwestern No. 120, North British No. 256, "Glen Douglas," Great North of Scotland No. 49, "Gordon Highlander," and a "Dunalastair" class engine, number unavailable.
Former Great Northern locomotives still serving on the U.T.A.

NETHERLANDS: **Utrecht:** Spoorwegmuseum. Nederlandse Rhijn Spoorweg No. 107, built in 1889.

NORWAY: **Hamar:** Jernbanemuseet. N.S.B. No. 7, built 1901.

Americans, Plain and Fancy

The first American type was designed by Henry R. Campbell in 1836. While this engine itself could not be considered a success, nevertheless it set the stage for a highly successful type of locomotive. From an old print

41

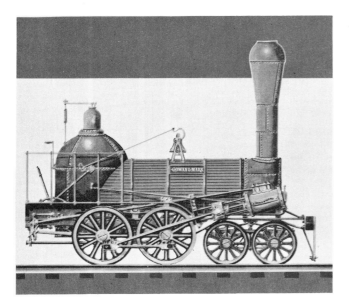

The "Gowan and Marx," built by Eastwick and Harrison in 1839, hauled a record load of 101 cars, 423 long tons from Reading to Philadelphia at ten miles per hour, on February 20, 1840. This record achievement made the 4-4-0 type popular almost overnight.

Author's collection

Built by the Boston designer, Seth Wilmarth, about 1849, the "Fury" was one of the first locomotives to have a cab.   New York Central

The oldest 4-4-0 in existence, built around 1840, the People's Railway #3, now rests in the Franklin Institute in Philadelphia. The cab and the lights were probably added around 1850.   Franklin Institute

The artist was right; this early 4-4-0 did have slanted cylinders. Built by Lancaster (Pa.) Locomotive Works.
From an old print

Lack of the standard Currier & Ives imprint (on all their prints after 1856), and the absence of a headlight, indicate that this locomotive was built around 1850. Note also the unusual tender wheel arrangement. N. Currier

To celebrate the opening of the then longest rail line in America, the Erie Railroad arranged a 427-mile junket on May 14, 1851. Included among the guests were President Millard Fillmore, several members of his cabinet, and Daniel Webster. Webster, pictured here, believed it unsafe to ride in a closed car and brought along his own rocking chair to ride the flat car the railroad provided him. General Motors

A Rock Island 4-4-0 crosses the first railroad bridge across the Mississippi at Davenport, Iowa. This bridge featured in a year-long lawsuit between railroad and steamboat interests, which was won for the Rock Island by a country lawyer, Abraham Lincoln. General Motors

A remarkably successful passenger locomotive designed by James Millholland, the "Hiawatha" had an unusual all-iron cab with round walls and a dome top. This engine set a new record of 720,727 miles traveled for the Reading Railroad before it retired in 1883.
Reading

43

The "Roanoke"—named after the county since there was no town of Roanoke until 1882—was typical of freight engines on the Virginia & Tennessee in the 1850's. Placed in service in January, 1854, it was the eighth engine on the road and with its tender weighed 39 tons ready to go. Norfolk and Western

Running board design and cab style indicate this is probably a Seth Wilmarth design. This locomotive of the Walkill Valley Railroad (later NYC) was the first to reach Ulster Co., N.Y. New York Central

44

The 4-4-0 as a villain: antirailroad posters like this were often financed by the worried canal boat operators.
Pennsylvania Railroad

The Utica Head Light Works was one of many independent manufacturers who made headlights for the railroads. This box light is typical of those used on 4-4-0's in the 1860's. Old advertisement

Very soon railroads were taking business from the canals. This was particularly true when railroads paralleled the canals and the speeding freights left the canal boats far behind. This picture was taken at the Delaware and Raritan Canal, a part of the extensive canal system of the East. Trenton Free Public Library

William Mason combined art with the locomotive builders craft. The "James Guthrie," built in 1852, was his first locomotive. Originally delivered to the Louisville, Cincinnati and Lexington (later L. & N.), it was acquired by the U.S. Military Railroad, in 1863. Louisville and Nashville

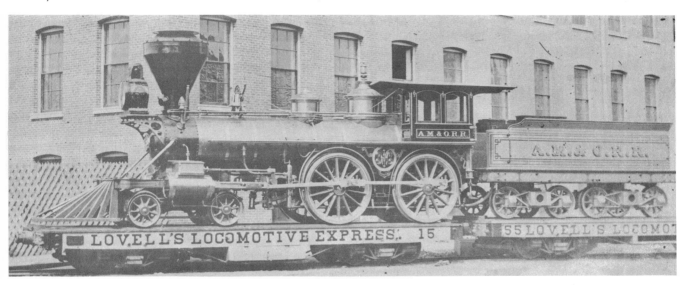

This William Mason locomotive was on its journey from Taunton, Mass., to the Atlantic, Mississippi and Ohio Railroad (now Norfolk & Western). The flat cars were probably bought by Mason when the Lovell company ceased operating. Note the exquisite Mason "signature" between the driving wheels. Merle K. Peirce

45

B. & O.'s No. 25 "William Mason" was the first for the B. & O. by William Mason. Built in 1856, this engine is now in the B. & O. Transportation Museum, Mt. Clare Station, Baltimore, Maryland.

Baltimore and Ohio

The "Highland Light" best designed engine of the 1860's and William Mason's outstanding creation—this is the opinion of many locomotive fanciers. Built in 1867 for the Cap Cod Central (later Old Colony Railroad, still later New Haven Railroad).

N. H. Photo-Michael R. Miller Collection

An Orange and Alexandria Railroad locomotive confiscated by the government during the Civil War. Built by William Mason in 1863, it was named for the first chief of the Military Railway Service, General Haupt. Note the intricate designs put on the engine even though the country was in a state of emergency.

National Archives - Brady Collection

Railroads and the 4-4-0's, such as this Baldwin product, played a decisive role in the winning of the Civil War. The North with its superior rail power easily outmaneuvered the South in the movement of troops and supplies.

National Archives - Brady Collection

After the battle: the crew of this U.S. Military Railroad point out mortar holes in the tank and the stack, and the dome knocked askew—results of a Civil War engagement. Note the link and pin coupler.

National Archives - Brady Collection

47

An American type of the U.S. Military Railroad on the Potomac Creek Bridge. This bridge, constructed in 1862 under General Herman Haupt's supervision, was built by unskilled soldiers using trees cut in nearby woods, in nine working days. It stood almost 100 ft. high and was about 400 ft. long. President Lincoln, describing it to his War Committee, said, ". . . And, upon my word, gentlemen, there is nothing in it but bean poles and cornstalks."

Association of American Railroads

The "General," hero of "The Great Locomotive Chase," as it appeared around 1891.

Louisville and Nashville

48

The "General," fully restored and under steam during the 1964-65 Civil War Centennial.

Louisville and Nashville

Even though it ran backward all the way, the "Texas" was able to capture the "General" after an eight-hour chase. Louisville and Nashville

This monument in Chattanooga, Tennessee, National Cemetery, commemorates the Andrew's Raiders and the stealing of the "General." Chattanooga Chamber of Commerce

A study in contrasts: the famous "General" stands beside a General Motors G.P.30 diesel. General Motors

Lincoln's Funeral Train with Pennsylvania Railroad engine #331 draped in black and flying American flags.

Pennsylvania Railroad

Another view of Pennsylvania Railroad #331 decorated for the sad task of pulling Lincoln's Funeral Train.

Pennsylvania Railroad

Long before this picture in 1893, Louisville and Nashville #17 pulled the funeral train of the only Confederate President, Jefferson Davis. In memory of this event, she continued to carry the Confederate star for many years.

Louisville and Nashville R. R.

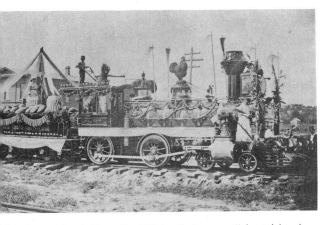

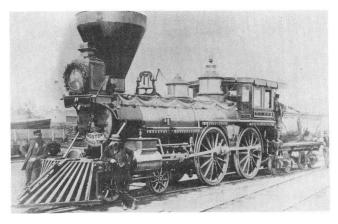

The Santa Fe Railroad's "Little Buttercup," lavishly decorated in 1880 for a festival event.   Santa Fe

The "Ruby," built in 1870 by Rogers of Paterson, N.J.
Shown decorated for a Boston Board of Trade Western
tour.   New York Central

The "America," popularly known as the "Silver Engine." The boiler of this 4-4-0 was covered with a jacket of
German silver while its trimmings—handles, whistle, pump, flagstaffs, and headlight brackets—were of pure silver.
                                                                                          Rock Island

51

The "John M. Forbes," a Baldwin locomotive built for the Philadelphia, Wilmington & Baltimore Railroad in 1866. The engine was named for John Murray Forbes who later became a Burlington director for many years. Note the curved windows.

Burlington

In 1871 Thatcher Perkins designed the "Southern Belle," No. 29. This beautiful engine, built by the Louisville and Nashville shops, was later celebrated in the old Southern ballad, "The 29."

Louisville and Nashville

"Tennessee No. 1"—pride of the North Carolina and St. Louis Railroad in the late 1890's and early 1900's. This trim 4-4-0 was used exclusively to pull the private car of the line's president, Major John W. Thomas.

Louisville and Nashville

The Pennsylvania Railroad station at Harrisburg, Pa., in 1861. Already a thriving passenger and freight center, it certainly was a good place to watch 4-4-0's.   Pennsylvania Railroad

First train to arrive in Peewee Valley, Ky., in 1867, on the Louisville, Cincinnati and Lexington (later Louisville & Nashville) Railroad. This 4-4-0 is probably #5, built by Hinkley in 1851.   Louisville and Nashville

No. 2 of the Meadville, Conneaut Lake and Linesville Railway (later Bessemer and Lake Erie) at the Meadville, Pa., station.

Bessemer and Lake Erie

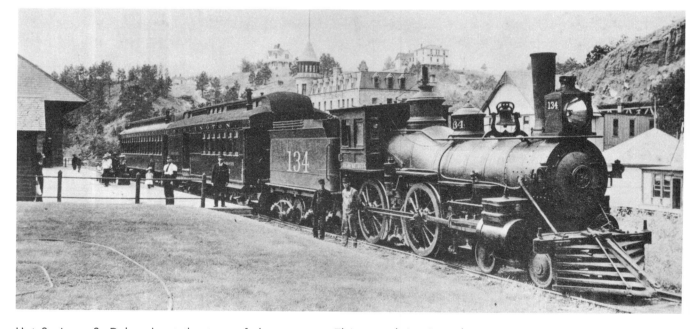

Hot Springs, S. Dak., about the turn of the century. This nostalgic view shows No. 134 of the Burlington and Missouri River, now the C.B. & Q.

Burlington

The first coal burner, "Irvington," was introduced by the Hudson River Railroad in 1852.

New York Central

No. 13, a Pennsylvania Railroad D 1, was the first locomotive to be equipped with George Westinghouse's new "atmospheric brakes" in 1869.

Westinghouse Air Brake

The "Pennsylvania Limited," pulled by a D-13, was the first completely electric lighted train in the United States, in 1892. This photograph shows the "Limited" on the iron truss bridge over the Susquehanna River at Rockville, near Harrisburg.

Pennsylvania Railroad

A forerunner of the famous Freedom Train was the Corn Train sent from Wichita, Kans., to the Ohio Valley after a severe flood there in 1884. Harpers Weekly

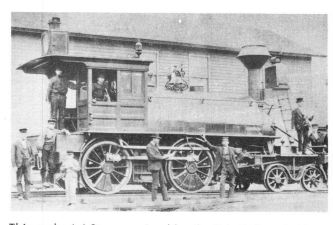

This early 4-4-0t was owned by the Erie Railroad. Note the two lights, the ladder on the front, and the ornate bell bracket. Rail Photo Service

Eugene Fontaine's engine actually made 90 miles per hour on a test run in Michigan. But railroad men did not appreciate the fact that speed was gained at the expense of pulling power. Fontaine's experiments were written off as impractical. The two prototypes were changed into conventional 4-4-0's. Author's collectoion

The Soo Line provided a 4-4-0 for Holman's first experiment. Baldwin built a second one new. "Holman's Absurdities" ended when both engines got their wheels back on the rails as standard Americans. Soo Line

The famous meeting at Promontory Point of balloon-stacked "Jupiter," No. 60 of the Central Pacific and No. 119 of the Union Pacific with straight stack. These 4-4-0's met to celebrate the completion of the first transcontinental railroad. Part of this event, of course, was the driving of a golden spike into a laurel tie.

Southern Pacific

Union Pacific's cap-stacked #119, their 4-4-0 celebrant at Promontory Point.

Southern Pacific

No. 119 was still around in 1909, this photo taken on September 4 of that year at O'Fallons, Nebr. William L. Colburn

The "Jupiter" Central Pacific's engine on its way to the Promontory Point celebration.

Southern Pacific

"No. 110," built by Watkeys of Syracuse, N.Y., was used to run the Sunday newspaper from New York to Buffalo in eleven hours. With an average speed of 50 mph over the 470 miles, this run became the inspiration for the "Fast Mail" service.

Harpers Weekly

Burlington Railroad's "Fast Mail" train was inaugurated between Chicago and Council Bluffs, Omaha, in 1884. Average speed: 31 mph.

Burlington

A rare photo of the famous "999" showing the large drivers, later reduced in size. On May 10, 1893, the "999" broke all existing speed records at 112½ mph. Today this engine can be seen at Chicago's Museum of Science and Industry.

New York Central

The famous "999" in action scooping water from a New York Central track pan.

New York Central

One of the most deluxe express trains was the New Haven "White Train." It was decorated in creamy white and gold trim and had gold upholstery on its furniture. This 4-4-0 ran with whitewashed coal and a white-uniformed crew.

New Haven

One of the first Oregon and California Railroad locomotives on the bridge across the Clakamas River. The photo was taken shortly after the first 20-mile section of the railroad was completed out of Portland and placed in operation on December 25, 1869.

Southern Pacific

The Oregon and California Railroad's Grave Creek trestle, built in 1883, with a work train.

Southern Pacific

Old Number 1, "General Sherman," granddaddy of all motive power on the Union Pacific. This shiny wood burner was built by Danforth & Cooke of Paterson, N.J., in 1864. It arrived in Omaha by steamboat in June, 1865.   Union Pacific

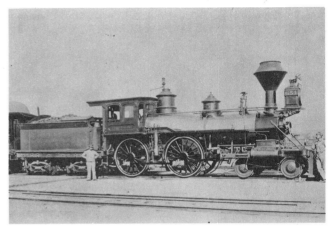

Hinkley and Williams completed this beauty for the U.P. roster in 1869. It was numbered 156, renumbered 654, and renumbered once more 486.   Union Pacific

The Bloomer Cut, near Auburn, Calif., on the original Central Pacific line over the Sierras, stands today much like it was when this picture was taken in 1867. Fourteen thousand Chinese coolies chopped cuts, like this, and tunnels through conglomerate as hard as concrete.
                                        Southern Pacific

No. 815 of the Union Pacific was built by Taunton in 1875, served until 1923.   Union Pacific

The "Seminole," wood-burning locomotive built in April, 1867, by Rogers for the U.P.R.R. Eastern District (Kans.). Overall length, 50 ft.; weight, 115,000 lbs.; fuel capacity, two cords; tender capacity, 2,000 gallons water; tractive power, 11,000 lbs. The cab of the old "Seminole" was of varnished walnut and the engineer's seat was made of ash.

Union Pacific

Showy antlers and shiny brass reflect the love some engineer devoted to this Schenectady-built 4-4-0, No. 23 on the Union Pacific.

Union Pacific

Santa Fe's No. 5, "Thomas Sherlock," built in 1870 by the Taunton Locomotive Works at a cost of $5,800, was scrapped in 1911 after 41 years of service.

Santa Fe

Forerunner of the Zip Code! In 1901 the Santa Fe renumbered its low number engines with an 0 prefix.   Santa Fe

A Pennsylvania D13c—Class P engine produced by the Altoona Shops in 1893.   Pennsylvania R. R.

No. 325 was one of 21 such Baldwin engines built for the Pennsylvania in 1864. Behind the rear driver is a friction wheel for the "Loughridge chain brake." P. R. R.

This Pennsylvania Railroad locomotive with a permanently attached coach was the ancestor of the modern self-propelled rail cars. Built in 1861, No. 217 was Baldwin's 1,000th locomotive.   Pennsylvania R. R.

Alco built this engine in 1903 for the St. Louis, Vandalia and Terre Haute Railroad. The Vandalia later became Pennsy's St. Louis Division.   Alfred E. Barker

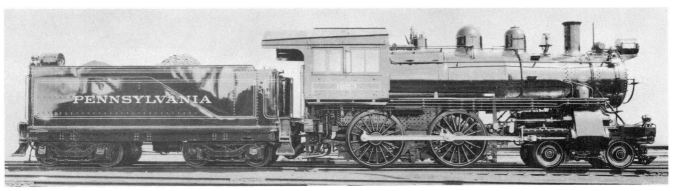

65

Pennsylvania's D16sb's were famous for sustained high-speed running. No. 1223 is now preserved at Strasburg, Pa.   Pennsylvania R. R.

No. 5079, a Pennsylvania D16sb leased to the Baltimore and Eastern Railroad was used until 1950.   William V. Russell

Old No. 1, pride of the Lynchburg and Durham Railroad Co. Headlights were ordered separate from the loco-motive.
Norfolk and Western

Norfolk and Western locomotive No. 502, a **Rogers** product of Civil War vintage. Note back-up light on cab roof.
Norfolk and Western

Sunday outings for the railroaders and their wives and sweethearts were common around the turn of the century. This picnic was held in N. & W.'s mountainous terrain.
Norfolk and Western

The "Edward Kidder" was a 32-ton wood-burning passenger engine built by William Mason in 1886 for the Wilmington and Weldon Railroad.
Atlantic Coast Line

This American-type passenger engine served the Jacksonville, St. Augustine and Indian River Railroad in the 1890's.

Alfred E. Barker

Georgia Southern and Florida's No. 151 was a product of the Schenectady Locomotive Works.

Alfred E. Barker

In 1852, 1,378 cars of mail, passengers, and freight crossed the frozen Susquehanna River pulled across by engines stationed on the shores.

Pennsylvania R. R.

Narrow-gauge engine No. 22 of the Cody & Moore Railroad tries out the ice in Central Michigan in 1885.

E. W. Langford

Eight Central Pacific 4-4-0's labored together behind a bucker plow keeping the Sierra Nevada's Donner Pass open during the winter of 1870.

Southern Pacific

Diamond-stacked No. 1 on the narrow-gauge South Pacific Coast Railroad as pictured in Oakland, Calif.   Alfred E. Barker

South Pacific Coast No. 9 and combine in a sylvan setting.   Alfred E. Barker

This South Pacific Coast American turned over after making kindling wood out of a preceding train.   Alfred E. Barker

No. 12 on the Old Colony Railroad was the "Nathaniel Thayer" built by Rogers in 1867.

The George Eastman House Collection

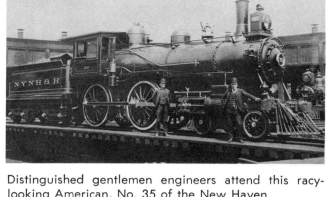

Distinguished gentlemen engineers attend this racy-looking American, No. 35 of the New Haven.

Merle K. Peirce

No. 125 of the Old Colony Railroad poses on the Spring Street turntable in New Haven, in the late 1870's.

N. H. Photo Michael R. Miller Collection

1864: The first Old Colony train passes through the Mt. Carmel cut.

N. H. Photo Michael R. Miller Collection

An Old Colony 4-4-0 and train on the wooden bridge at Fair Haven. The bridge, built in 1852, was replaced in 1890.

N. H. Photo Michael R. Miller Collection

The "Falmouth" of the Old Colony Railroad was Mason creation quite similar to the "Highland Light" of 1867.   The George Eastman House Collection

New York, Providence and Boston Railroad's No. 16 was equipped with an unusual spark arrestor.   N. H. Photo Michael R. Miller Collection

Old Colony Railroad's No. 157 was built by the Taunton Machine Works, Taunton, Mass., around 1880.

The George Eastman House Collection

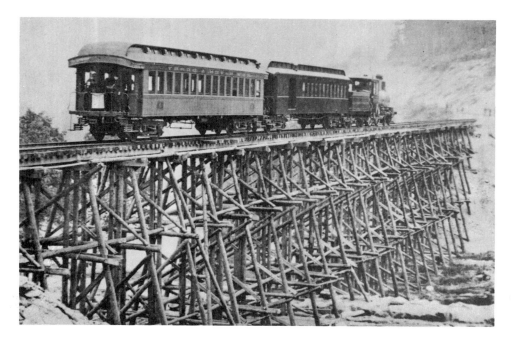

New Haven and Derry Railroad 4-4-0 and two wooden coaches on a trestle near Derry, Conn., about 1885.

Rail Photo Service

A West River Train pulled by No. 33 about to leave Londonderry, Vt.   Rail Photo Service

Rutland Railroad's No. 244 was built by Brooks of Dunkirk in 1900. Note the Fox trucks under the tender.

Alfred E. Barker

In 1880 John Wootten designed the anthracite-burning camelback-type locomotive for the Reading Railroad. This 4-4-0w with 43.8 tons service weight was one of the heaviest passenger engines of its day.   Reading

The American Locomotive Company produced a large class of engines like the 937 for the Lackawanna around 1905. A few of this series were rebuilt about 1938 with cabs at the rear and a semi-streamlined design.

Erie-Lackawanna

73

This Lackawanna Camelback was still busy in 1948.
William L. Colburn

A Reading 4-4-0w, built in the home shops in 1911, served faithfully until 1940.   William L. Colburn

Not all camelbacks stayed East. Rogers built ten 4-4-0w's for the Union Pacific in 1887.

Union Pacific

Union Pacific's ten-wheeler No. 1277 and camelback No. 766 doubleheading the express across a spidery trestle.

Union Pacific

This 4-4-0 camelback, No. 952 of the Lackawanna, is preserved in St. Louis, Mo.   National Museum of Transport

Practically all Northeastern Pennsylvania, New York, and New Jersey railroads owned camelbacks. This is No. 27 of the Staten Island Railway, built by the American Locomotive Co.   American Locomotive

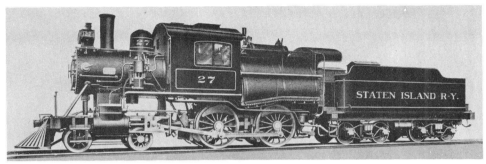

A Burlington doubleheader near Mendota, Ill., in 1899.

Burlington

Burlington's No. 25 heading a suburban train in 1880. Note the paint scheme on smokebox. Burlington

Beautifully detailed was No. 49, a Schenectady-built 4-4-0 delivered to the Louisiana, New Orleans and Texas Railway in 1898. Alfred E. Barker

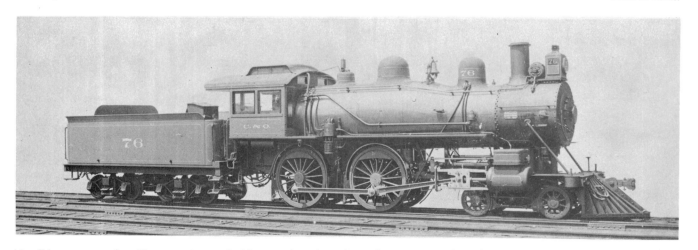

No. 76 came to the Chesapeake and Ohio Railroad with a clerestory roof and a steam generator. Alfred E. Barker

Eleven Americans and one Mogul, totaling 854 tons, were used to test this Central Vermont Railroad bridge at Hartford, Vt., in 1887.

John Roebling, wire maker and bridge builder, built this bridge across the Niagara chasm in 1854.

Canadian National

The Whirlpool Rapids Bridge across the Niagara, built in 1897, replaced an earlier single-track suspension bridge built by the famous John Roebling in 1854.
Canadian National

78

A train of the Canada Southern, later the New York Central, at Falls View Station near Niagara Falls, 1855.
New York Central

The "Trevithick," of the Grand Trunk Railway, was built in 1859, and in 1860 hauled the Royal Train of the Prince of Wales, later King Edward VII. Canadian Pacific

No. 285 was the first engine built by the Canadian Pacific Railway Shops in Montreal. Note the straight boiler. Canadian Pacific

No. 29, another product of the C. P. Montreal Shops, ser ved 73 years and two months. Built in 1887, it has been preserved to this day.
Canadian Pacific

4-4-0's were rare in the logging empires. Here we see a cabbage stack 4-4-0 of the Dowling & Camp Lumber Co. Railroad at Slater, Fla., 1939.

Bethlehem Cornwall Corporation

Chehalis County Logging and Timber Co. Railroad No. 12 at Montesano, Wash., moving a load of logs across a timber trestle.

John T. Labbe Collection

80

Algoma Lumber Company No. 1506, a Baldwin of 1872, working north of Klamath Falls, Oreg. J.T. Labbe

Another view of Chehalis County Logging and Timber Co.'s No. 12.

John T. Labbe Collection

A beautiful setting frames a nameless 4-4-0 of the Silverton Lumber Co. in Oregon.

Oregon Historical Society

No. 3 on the Silverton Lumber Co., Silverton, Oregon.

Oregon Historical Sosiety

81

Traded more times than a professional ballplayer, this 4-4-0 was built by the Schenectady Locomotive Works as No. 12 of the Adirondack and St. Lawrence. Later it became Central Vermont's No. 233, New York Central's 863, Rutland's 83, and Fort Smith and Western's 4.

Alfred E. Barker

The "Penryn" (Baldwin 1889) took care of the passenger business on the iron ore hauling Cornwall Railroad in eastern Pennsylvania.
Bethlehem Corwall Corporation

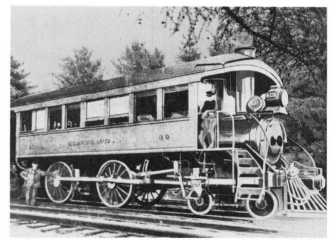

Practically all major railroads had a few American types rebuilt into inspection engines for their officials. Here we see New York Central's No. 30, the "Cleveland."
New York Central

The Mount Gretna Narrow Gauge Railway, a subsidiary of the Cornwall Railroad, owned the only two-foot-gauge Americans ever built. Of these, No. 12 was constructed in a record time of eight days.   Bethlehem Cornwall Corporation

Boston and Albany's inspection engine "Berkshire."   New York Central

In 1927 this Great Northern engine worked around St. Paul, Minnesota.   William L. Colburn

No. 933 of the Boston and Maine takes on water in Beverly, Mass., in 1941. Note the low headlight on this Brooks product.   William L. Colburn

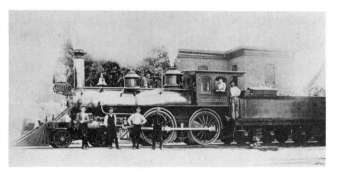

No. 2 on Ohio's Scioto Valley Line, now a part of the Norfolk and Western.   Norfolk and Western

Soo Line's tall-stacked No. 25, with cab curtains and wooden pilot as seen at St. Paul, Minn., in 1934.
William L. Colburn

The six-spot of the Middletown and Unionville Railroad has just taken on coal and water for a day's work in Orange County, N.Y.   William L. Colburn

No. 135 of the Houston and Texas Central: simple, sturdy, and capable.

Alfred E. Barker

The Manchester and Oneida Railway No. 6 had an unusual pilot plow. William L. Colburn

William A. Keefer

William L. Colburn

The Chesapeake Beach Railroad of Maryland ceased operations in 1935. But several of its engines, which had already served four previous owners, continued their useful existence on the East Washington Railroad until 1946.

No. 1 of the Kansas City, Pittsburg and Gulf was built by Baldwin in 1895. When the line was reorganized, No. 1 became Kansas City Southern No. 107.
Kansas City Southern

No. 2 of the Kansas City, Fort Smith and Southern built by Brooks in 1889, became K.C.P. & G. No. 10, later K.C.S. No. 132.
Kansas City Southern

The year is 1933, and Kansas City Southern No. 140, an oil burner, rests at Lake Charles, La.
William L. Colburn

No. 200 of the Missouri, Kansas, Texas, the "Katy Flyer," built in 1890, was later converted into an oil burner.
Missouri Kansas Texas

Nos. 1, 2, 3, 4, 479, and 492 formed Class F1 of the Atlantic Coast Line. Rogers built these wood burners in 1885.

Atlantic Coast Line

One of the Lackawanna Camelbacks, No. 988, was rebuilt as a conventional type with imaginative "stream-lining."

Erie-Lackawanna

Coaling up is No. 91 of the Chicago and North Western. This class A passenger engine was built at Schenectady in 1895.

Chicago and North Western

This builder's photo of a Chicago & North Western Class A passenger engine shows how No. 91 might have looked before any changes or additions were made during its half century of service.

Alfred E. Barker

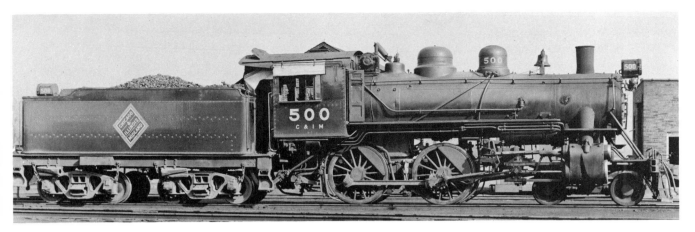

Engines No. 500 and 501 for the Chicago and Illinois Midland were the last 4-4-0's built for an American railroad. They were delivered by Baldwin 1927-28.
Chicago and Illinois Midland

No. 500 in a later paint scheme.
William L. Colburn

The 500 and 501 of the Chicago & Illinois Midland quit running in March 1954, ending 118 years of 4-4-0 service on main line railroads.
Chicago and Illinois Midland

This trim-looking 4-4-0 with its long low tender was delivered by Alco to the Lake Erie, Franklin & Clarion Railroad, a Pennsylvania short line.
William L. Colburn

No. 121, one of the workhorses of the coal-hauling Delaware and Hudson Railroad.

Alfred E. Barker

Daily except Sunday this rather British-looking 4-4-0 hauled a three-car Delaware and Hudson local out of Saratoga Springs, N.Y.

Frank Quin

Many 4-4-0's spent their latter days on work trains. This Kansas City Southern engine is assigned to the pile driver.

Kansas City Southern

To Minneapolis and Rainy River No. 12 fell the sad task of removing the rails in 1932.   William L. Colburn

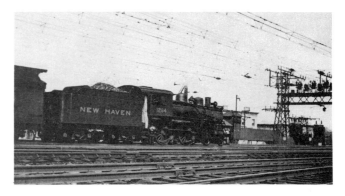

New Haven's 1284 with cab curtains pulled the wire train till well after World War II.   Ed Wadhams

"Make way for ducklings!" A Crown Metal two-foot gauge engine crosses the Loyalhanna Creek near Ligonier, Pa.
McKeesport Daily News

This Crown Metal two-footer runs on the grounds of
the Hawthorn Mellody Farms, Libertyville, Ill.
Crown Metal Products Co.

A.D. 1965! A three-foot-gauge replica of Civil War
vintage built by the Crown Metal Products Co. of
Wyano, Pa.
Crown Metal Products Co.

Two views of a 30-inch gauge replica of Union Pacific's famous Golden Spike engine No. 119, built for the
Henry Doorley Zoo, Omaha, Nebraska by Crown Metal.
Crown Metal Products Co.

Portland Zoo No. 1, the "Oregon," is a beautiful
replica built in 1959 by a group of local enthusiasts.
John T. Labbe

Gleaming Domes: a view from the fireman's side. Jan Gleysteen

Locomotive No. 7 of the Egersund-Flekkefjord Railway in Norway, built in 1901. It is preserved in operating condition at Hamar.
Norges Statsbaner

No. 30 of the Norwegian State Railways was built by Nydquist and Holm in Sweden, 1878. Norges Statsbaner

A Class C engine of the Danish State Railways. Like the South Funen engine below, its stack carries the national colors.
Danske Statsbanerne

A happy combination of American and European features is found in this engine of the South Funen Railway of Denmark. Danske Statsbanerne

No. 67, built by Baldwin for the narrow-gauge division of the Ferrocarrilles Unidos de Yucatan, Mexico. A. E. Barker

No. 67 as she appears today after 60 years of service.

Edgar T. Mead, Jr.

No. 351, Baldwin 1887, about to leave Progreso in August, 1963.

J. David Conrad

No. 5 of the standard gauge division of the F.F.C.C. Unidos de Yucatan, a Baldwin graduate of 1887.

Edgar T. Mead, Jr.

The last 4-4-0 built in the U.S., delivered by Baldwin to the Yucatan in 1946.

Author's Collection

The "Lenzburg" of the Swiss Nordostbahn, built by Krauss-Maffei in 1861, ended its career in 1903.

Verkehrshaus der Schweiz, Luzern

The "Sarine" served three Swiss companies between 1862 and 1901. The cab affords little protection from the Alpine snows.

Verkehrshaus der Schweiz, Luzern

Another Swiss tank engine: Jura-Simplon Bahn No. 33. Built in Esslingen, Germany, in 1891, it was in service until 1925.

Verkehrshaus der Schweiz, Luzern

No. 107 of the Nederlandse Rhijn Spoorweg, built by North British Locomotive Co., Glasgow, as it appears today at the Museum in Utrecht, Holland.

Jan Gleysteen

Nederlandse Centraal Spoorweg No. 41, with white tires, brass dome, and cap stack, was in service from 1899-1950.

Nederlandse Spoorwegen

Between 1889 and 1907 Beyer Peacock delivered 135 of these inside-connected 4-4-0's to the Dutch Railways.

Nederlandse Spoorwegen

Hollandse Spoorweg Maatschappij 505, later 2100 on the nationalized system, was one of 70 such machines. Built in the company shops from 1914 on, they were the largest 4-4-0's of their day.

Nederlandse Spoorwegen

Both Belgium and Spain used long engine numbers, such as the stenciled 18059 on the smokebox of this T18 class engine of the Etat-Belge.

Belgische Spoorweg Maatschappy

This Italian creation of 1899, an express passenger engine, won a citation of merit for design at the 1900 International Exhibit in Paris.

F. S. Italia

95

Italian engines, practically always home-built, fell victim to endless experimenting and tests. As a result no two engines of the same class, in this case GR106, ever quite looked alike.

F. S. Italia

The "City of Truro," speed queen of the British Isles, restored in the original Great Western colors, now rests in the museum at Swindon.

British and Irish Railways, Inc.

One of the greatest classes of 4-4-0's, the "Dunalastair," was born in the Caledonian Railway Shops in Glasgow. Named after a Scottish estate, it was foremost in efficiency, robustness, and power output in relation to size.

Dr. G. P. Stilley

A Dunalastair IV of the Caledonian Railway popping off at the Princess Street Station in Edinburgh. The miniature semaphore on the buffer beam indicates this engine is going to and from the north out of Edinburgh Princess Street.

Dr. G. P. Stilley

No. 86, a graceful 4-4-0 of the North Stafford Railway, built at Stoke-on-Trent in 1910. From an old postcard

The "Butler Henderson," No. 56 of the Great Central, was one of the 44 Directors Class engines built in 1913. It is now preserved in London.   R. Peover

A Schools Class 4-4-0 wheeling an express train out of London in 1955.
British and Irish Railways, Inc.

A long way from home! Baldwin built this engine for the New South Wales Railways of Australia in 1877.

Dept. of Railways, N. S. W.

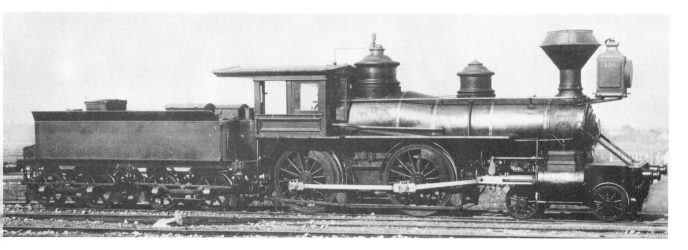

One of six Beyer Peacock 4-4-0t's placed in service on the New South Wales Railways in 1880. All were later converted to tender types. In 1913 they were sold to the Commonwealth Railways for construction of the Trans-Australian line. Dept. of Railways, N. S. W.

The Vulcan Foundry of Lancashire, England, built this engine in 1887 for the New South Wales Railways.
Dept. of Railways, N. S. W.

98

New South Wales Railways Z12-type locomotive as delivered by Beyer Peacock in 1878.
Dept. of Railways, N. S. W.

A Z12 class engine in later years. The most obvious improvement is the cab with a porthole window.
Dept. of Railways, N. S. W.

Cast iron toys practically always followed the popular 4-4-0 prototype.

Kauffman Museum, N. Newton, Kansas

A Märklin live steam model of 1902.

Märklin, GmbH

A free-lance model in O gauge by William Danner for his Rockland and Western Railroad.

William Danner

Little Engines, Inc., of Lomita, Calif., manufactures these beautiful backyard steamers.

Jan Gleysteen

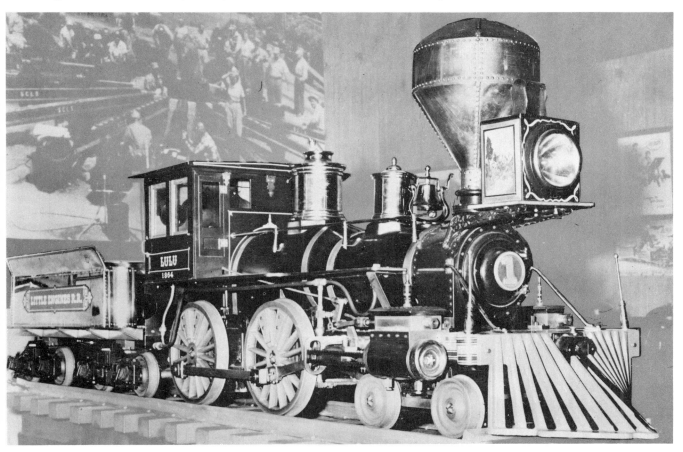

99

A coal-fired model of the Dunalastair II class No. 777 of the Caledonian Railway, weighing 66 lbs., in working order.

Dr. G. P. Stilley

The "City of Truro" in miniature, by Kitmaster.

Paul M. Schrock

This straight-boilered locomotive in O gauge was manufactured by Thomas of Shawnee, Oklahoma. P. M. Schrock

Lionel's rendition of the famous "General."

Paul M. Schrock

Rev. Larry C. Jewell scratch-built this HO model based on Southern Pacific characteristics.

Paul M. Schrock

The "Genoa" of the Virginia and Truckee Railroad by AHM of Philadelphia passes a Mantua "General" on the lower level.

Paul M. Schrock

The "William Crooks," an O gauge model by Marx.

Paul M. Schrock

Strictly British: A class 3P 4-4-0 of the British Railways by Triang followed by a Schools Class engine by Kit-master.

Paul M. Schrock

This still life illustrates the occurrence of the 4-4-0 on greeting cards and pie plates, in toys and models, paperweights—yes, even a bar of soap!

Paul M. Schrock

Nearly two hundred hours of embroidery went into the making of this sampler. Only a color reproduction would reveal the fine nuances of color used to achieve depth and dimension.

Gerrie Gleysteen

Between 1854 and 1857 around 300 million dollars of railroad money was issued, much of it decorated with American types in action. Author's Collection

Two of the many stamps featuring 4-4-0's: to the left Baldwin's first engine for the Finnish Railways in 1862; to the right Chilean Railway's first engine built by Rogers in 1851. Author's Collection

The eight-wheeler in the fine arts: the "American Express Train" drawn by Nathaniel Currier in 1855. Nathaniel Currier

Atlantic and Great Western locomotive No. 71 is thought to have modeled for this Currier and Ives lithograph of
1870.

Currier and Ives

104

"The 9:45 Accommodation, Stratford, Connecticut" by Henry Edward Lamson, 1867.

Metropolitan Museum of Art

This wire sculpture by an unknown artist with much patience was found in an antique shop in Barcelona, Spain.

Richard Westerman

"Train to Trinidad" by Otto Kuhler, 1964. The engine is a Colorado and Wyoming Railroad 4-4-0.   Otto Kuhler

This charming pen drawing of an old 4-4-0 in the summer sun is also by Otto Kuhler.   Otto Kuhler

Dee Flagg, the great Arizona sculptor, made this 40-foot bas-relief of "Jesse James' Last Great Train Robbery—1881" after months of research. The original is now owned by a Missouri businessman.   Dee Flagg

This woodcut by the author shows an engine running light, perchance going home after a busy day.   Jan Gleysteen

"Frontier Freight—1880" by Howard Fogg. An excellent watercolor showing action in the desert. W. H. Miner, Inc.

"Locomotive Speed King." The famous 999 and the Empire State Express are shown here in another one of Fogg's magnificent watercolors.

Pittsburgh and Lake Erie

No. 1 of the El Paso and South Western, preserved in El Paso, Texas (Texas Western College Campus), was built in 1859. El Paso Chamber of Commerce

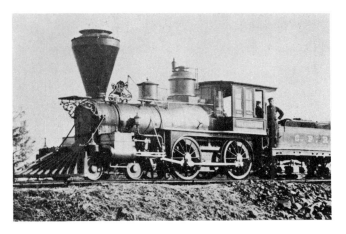

The "Governor Stanford" arrived in California in 1863 after a 15,000-mile trip around Cape Horn. Central Pacific's No. 1 now is preserved in San Francisco. Southern Pacific

The "William Crooks," No. 1 of the St. Paul and Pacific Railroad (now Great Northern), was built in Paterson, N.J., in 1861. Beautifully restored, the engine is now on display in the St. Paul, Minnesota, Union Station. Great Northern

Built by Baldwin in 1872 for the Northern Pacific, the "Countess of Dufferin" arrived in Manitoba on a barge to become Canadian Pacific's No. 1. It is now on display in Winnipeg, Manitoba.
Canadian Pacific

Strikingly similar to the "Countess of Dufferin" was Morgan, Louisiana & Texas No. 44, here shown in the process of restoration in 1948. Unfortunately, No. 44 was stolen and presumably scrapped.   A. E. LaSalle

No. 1 of the Lake Shore and Michigan Southern, a Mason classic, now in the halls of the Henry Ford Museum.
                                    Henry Ford Museum

The "Sam Hill" of the Atlantic & Gulf Railroad, a Rogers product of 1860. One of four 4-4-0's in Henry Ford's Dearborn Collection.   Henry Ford Museum

Stockton Terminal and Eastern No. 1 was built in 1864 and retired in 1953 after 89 years of service. Griffith Park, Los Angeles, is her new home.   Jan Gleysteen

108

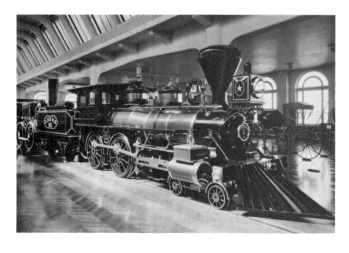

City of Winnipeg Hydro No. 3 was built in 1882 by Dubs of Glasgow, Scotland, for the Canadian Pacific. In 1918 it went to the Hydro, where it continued to run until 1964. Now in storage in Winnipeg.   Winnipeg Hydro

Walt Disney revives the past with this matchless replica, the "Cyrus K. Holliday," No. 1 on the Santa Fe Disneyland.   Jan Gleysteen

Spit and polish and parquet floors. Ford provides a home for Detroit, Toledo and Ironton's No. 7, built in 1897.   Henry Ford Museum

The youngest American in the Dearborn museum is No. 16 of the Toledo & Detroit Railroad, built by Baldwin in 1915.   Henry Ford Museum

Combining speed, power, and excellent design, Pennsylvania's D16 Americans are considered by many to be the best 4-4-0's ever built. No 1223 is now at Strasburg, Pa.   Lowell Detweiler

The charming Strasburg Rail Road, a must for rail fans, also owns this 1909 American, their No. 98, which came from the Louisiana & Eastern.   Jan Gleysteen

Texas II (ex-Talbottom Railroad No. 349) on the Stone Mountain Railroad in Georgia is used to chase the General II (ex-Louisiana & Eastern No. 1) when not posing with Southern Belles.   Stone Mountain Scenic Railroad

The "Sam Houston" No. 4 on the Southern Railway and Six Gun, Silver Springs, Fla.   Crown Metal

ACKNOWLEDGMENTS

Quite a number of years ago it occurred to me that no major effort had been made to document the development and achievements of what was undoubtedly the most common locomotive of them all—the 4-4-0 American type. An album with twenty-three photos and several magazine articles were the extent of the available materials.

Every historical publication is really a cooperative effort. The response to my author's queries in leading magazines was overwhelming and resulted in correspondence with about 200 persons or institutions during a four-year span. Thanks to their generous response, it soon became clear that the amount of information and photos received could never be incorporated in one single book. What you see before you is the cream of the crop.

The process of research and compiling was a gratifying experience. Some contributors, realizing the labor involved in preparing a book, kept on sending letters of encouragement. One busy medical doctor wrote a twenty-four-sheet letter, describing one locomotive. The reason why he didn't write more was that he was in the process of moving to a new home. A retired engineer from Texas kept sending weekly shipments of photos from his marvelous collection, always accompanied by a friendly note. A Rhode Island college student notified all his railroad friends of my needs, and as a result I have enough photos to do a book on New England 4-4-0's alone. The fine cooperation of the railroad companies, the Association of American Railroads, the museums, and historical collections around the country should also be mentioned. Only a few railroads, including some class I lines, did not bother to answer repeated letters. Another excellent source of photos was the Rail Photo Service of Boston, Massachusetts. To each one of those who have taken a lot of effort to help me develop this book, I express my heartfelt appreciation.

In addition to those who supplied data, there is another group that contributed much to this work. Crowding the top of this list of "others" are Paul M. Schrock, who edited, pruned, and sharpened up the original manuscript, Betty Krady and Kathryn Kreider who spent midnight and pre-dawn hours preparing the copy for the linotype, and John E. Harshberger, who is largely responsible for the design of this book. A word of praise to our copy-camera artist, Peteris V. Kalnins, responsible for the high quality offset photography. In many cases he was actually able to improve on the old and faded prints.

All accounts, information, statistics, and credits have been compared and checked as carefully as possible. You will find, as I have, that even company records and old newspapers have been known to be wrong, and if you are a perfectionist or a walking encyclopedia on a certain railroad, you will find that some of these errors have been transposed from supposedly reliable sources. Your corrections and additions will be appreciated.

Scottdale, Pa., Fall, 1965

Jan Gleysteen

BIBLIOGRAPHY

BALDWIN LOCOMOTIVE WORKS. Illustrated catalog, reprint. 154pp. Howell North, Berkeley, California. 1960.

CIVIL WAR RAILROADS. George B. Abdill. 192pp. Superior Publishing Co., Seattle, Washington. 1961.

COLLECTING MODEL TRAINS. Louis H. Hertz. 352pp. Simmons Boardman, New York City. 1956.

DIE DAMPFLOKOMOTIVE. Dr. Ing. F. Meineke. 520pp. Springer Verlag, Berlin. 1949.

IRON HORSES. E. P. Alexander. 240pp. W. W. Norton, New York. 1941.

LAND TRANSPORT No. III: RAILWAY LOCOMOTIVES AND ROLLING STOCK. E. A. Forward. 100pp. London: Her Majesty's Stationery Office. 1931.

LE FERROVIE ITALIANE DELLO STATO 1905-1955. 88pp. Direzione Generale delle F. S. Roma. 1955.

LITTLE RAILWAYS OF THE WORLD. Frederic Shaw. 262pp. Howell North. 1958.

LOCOMOTIEVEN VOORHEEN EN THANS. Dr. J. H. E. Reeskamp. 64pp. De Alk Beeld-Encyclopedie, Alkmaar, Holland. 1964.

LOCOMOTIVE ADVERTISING IN AMERICA, 1850-1900.

32pp. American Review, Scotia, New York. 1960.

LOCOMOTIVE CATECHISM. Robert Grimshaw, M.E. 438pp. Norman W. Henley, New York City. 1904.

LOCOMOTIVES OF THE PENNSYLVANIA RAILROAD 1834-1924. Paul T. Warner. 80pp. Owen Davies, Chicago. 1959.

ONZE NEDERLANDSE LOCOMOTIEVEN IN WOORD EN BEELD. H. Waldorp. 184pp. H. Stam, Haarlem, Holland. 1946.

PIONEER RAILROADS. Hank Wieand Bowman. 144pp. Fawcett Publications, Greenwich, Connecticut. 1954.

POPULAR MECHANICS RAILROAD ALBUM. John O'Connell. Popular Mechanics, Chicago. 1954.

RAILROAD PHOTO ALBUM No. 1: THE AMERICAN TYPE. Harry P. Albrecht. 48pp. Fox Schulman, Inc., Philadelphia. 1951.

RAILROADS IN THE DAYS OF STEAM. By the editors of American Heritage. 154pp. American Heritage Publishing Co., New York City. 1960.

RAILS WEST. George B. Abdill. 192pp. Superior Publishing Co. Seattle, Washington. 1960.

RAILWAYS. C. Hamilton Ellis. 156pp. Hulton Press, London. 1956.

SHORT HISTORY OF THE BALTIMORE AND OHIO RAILROAD. 48pp. Baltimore and Ohio Printing Dept. 1935.

THE FIRST QUARTER CENTURY OF STEAM LOCOMOTIVES IN NORTH AMERICA. Smith Hempstone Oliver. 114pp. Smithsonian Institute, Washington, D.C. 1956.

THE SANDLEY STORY. Frederic Shaw. 78pp. Hesperian House, San Francisco. 1960.

THE STEAM LOCOMOTIVE IN AMERICA. Alfred W. Bruce. 444pp. W. W. Norton. 1952.

THE TWILIGHT OF STEAM LOCOMOTIVES. Ron Ziel. 208pp. Grosset and Dunlap, New York City. 1963.

Magazines

TRAINS. Kalmbach Publishing Co., Milwaukee, Wisconsin.

RAILROAD. Popular Publications, New York, N.Y.

TRAINS ILLUSTRATED. Ian Allan Ltd., Surrey, Great Britain.

RAILWAY MAGAZINE. Tothill Press Ltd., London, Great Britain.

LA VIE DU RAIL. Editions N.M., Paris, France.

OP DE RAILS. N.V.B.S., Amsterdam, Holland.

Jan Gleysteen

112